HERITAGE *to* LEGACY

HERITAGE *to* LEGACY

PASSING ON STORIES OF FAITH

RUTH I CHRISTENSON

XULON PRESS

Xulon Press
2301 Lucien Way #415
Maitland, FL 32751
407.339.4217
www.xulonpress.com

Unless otherwise indicated, Scripture quotations taken from the New American Standard Bible (NASB). Copyright © 1960, 1962, 1963, 1968, 1971, 1972, 1973, 1975, 1977, 1995 by The Lockman Foundation. Used by permission. All rights reserved.

Paperback ISBN-13: 978-1-6628-1521-8

Ebook ISBN-13: 978-1-6628-1522-5

TABLE OF CONTENTS

Introduction

Heritage is defined as "the legacy of personal artifacts and intangible attributes of a group or society that are inherited from past generations, maintained in the present, and bestowed for the benefit of future generations." In the midst of day to day responsibilities, we don't often take the time to reflect on the past, nor appreciate the influence of faithful people in our lives. We also don't think about the long term legacy we too must leave. I hope the stories I share will inspire you to pause and look at the blessings of your own family, past and present. I pray that you will discover hidden treasures to share with your own loved ones. May all our stories be told, for the glory of God.

This book has been written to keep a promise to my adult children. Some of them are married and raising children of their own. They now find themselves using phrases they remember hearing from me. They want to know where these principles have their origin. Many of the related stories in this book are from our home, but there are certainly lessons I gleaned from many people in our lives. Sometimes, the words they spoke were audible. Often, the quiet daily example of living in obedience to God spoke loudest. Their testimonies of faith have become some of the treasures that we call our heritage. Though we are urged to work hard to leave a small financial inheritance for the next generation as a way to bless them, God tells us that riches can not follow any of us into eternity. We need to leave a legacy that has eternal value.

The first part of this book documents some of the family stories we have treasured. I believe God wants us to honor the memory of His work in past generations, so that we too will live lives of faith. Even more than the family heritage we enjoy, the Bible must always be the foundational influence for all of life. It contains the histories of many people who left a legacy of faithfulness from which we can learn. These people were not perfect, but their lives do reveal what happens when God is allowed to intervene in a home. There are also many families whose lives were filled with conflict and dysfunction. We can learn from them too. For the purpose of this book, I want to focus on positive attitudes and actions such as gratefulness, faith, and forgiveness.

Many chapters will contain examples from the Bible to help equip parents, including my own children, to see life from God's perspective. Mark 8:36 asks us, "... what does it profit a man to gain the whole world and forfeit his soul." I think that includes the souls of our families. Of all the things we can teach, loving and trusting the Lord is top priority. Let's be intentional to model that for our family and friends.

The last chapters of this book became a challenge to persevere and to live in this generation, with a bold testimony of God's faithfulness to us. We need encouragement to do this from other believers. We also need God's help to stand alone when necessary. Find the support you need, and be that person for someone else. It takes effort to connect. Pray for what my husband calls, "Divine Appointments." You will see God's hand at work in and through you.

I would like to thank those from our family's past, who are too many to name. Their daily lives of faith are still making an impact today. Thank you to my own family, whose stories and lessons have enriched my life and transformed my parenting. Most of all, thank you to the Lord, who is always active in our lives. His plan is still unfolding, and it is into His care we place the generations still to come.

Chapter 1

WHAT'S IN YOUR TREASURE BOX?

The picture that comes to my mind when I think about our heritage, our spiritual inheritance, is a treasure chest containing all the spiritual riches passed down from our ancestors. This treasure chest is a resource for this life, and one to which we certainly can add for generations to come.

King Solomon starts his collection of Proverbs with a similar image. "Hear, my son, your father's instruction, and do not forsake your mother's teaching. Indeed, they are a graceful wreath to your head and ornaments about your neck." (Proverbs 1:8) I am sure he heard his father, King David, and his mother, Bathsheba, sharing with him what they knew he would need to know to protect his life and reign. He would someday be king. What might they have said? Let me paraphrase a little. "Solomon, the wisdom you will need to be king begins with respect and obedience to God. Treasure wisdom. Search for it. Live and rule by it." I am sure that whenever they had a chance to have some continuing influence in his life, they reminded him to fear God.

They warned him about the temptations to sin that could destroy his life. Remember David and Bathsheba's immoral behavior led to a man's death, a baby's death, and a loss of respect for the authority of the king. Solomon was warned to beware of those who would lead him to take what didn't belong to him or to take advantage of those who were defenseless. Proverbs 1:10-14 warned him saying, "My son, if sinners entice you, do not consent. If they say, 'Come with us. Let us lie in wait for blood. Let us ambush the innocent without cause. ... We shall find all kinds of precious wealth. We shall fill our houses with spoil. Throw in your lot with us." What would be the consequences of such a life? Verse 18–19 says, "They lie in wait for their own blood; they ambush their own lives. So are the ways of everyone who gains by violence. It takes away the life of its possessors." Solomon's response would affect generations of his own family, and the nation he was responsible to protect.

So what is in our Treasure Box? Though there is much that is good in our collection of experiences, there may be other "items" that we could label as trash in our past: alcoholism (addictions), bitterness, grumbling, ingratitude, deceit, rebellion, and so on. Someone called these generational sins. We have the chance to look humbly at the struggles of our families and to turn to God who has the power to remove these weaknesses that could damage our relationships and legacy.

I remember a season in my home when there was a spirit of complaining. One child had something another child wanted. Then something wasn't going the way a third child expected, etc. I remember feeling the need to address what was becoming an undercurrent of grumbling. Have you noticed how contagious grumbling can become? God shows how seriously He disapproves of this attitude in the book of Numbers 21:1–9. Remember how the Children of Israel complained about food and water and leadership and the tedious wilderness journey they were on. God sent a plague of serpents among the people and many began to die from their poisonous bites.

Some of the people acknowledged their sin and asked Moses to speak to God on their behalf. The Lord said to make a bronze serpent, to hang it on a pole and to lift it up before the people. If a person was bit by a snake, he was to look up to that serpent as an act of believing that God would keep His promise to heal. That act of faith would lead to his life being spared. Those who confessed their sin, God forgave. They were saved.

I told this story to my children hoping they would understand that God hated grumbling. This attitude comes out of a heart that is not thankful nor content. Unfortunately, one of the younger children took the message so literally that she was terrified to go into our basement, because "there might be snakes there." I had to clarify that this happened years ago in Israel, but that God still wants us to trust Him and to be content with what He provides.

As often happens, God used a season like this one with my children to shine a spotlight on the grumbling that was happening in my own heart. I could complain with just a look on my face or a whisper under my breath. I realized I was modeling what I was trying to confront. It was my own sin God was addressing. I have asked many times since for forgiveness for grumbling, not just from God but from my family. I have found that practicing gratefulness replaces the complaining. I don't want the trash of a bad attitude to be left in our Family Treasure Box.

The Bible has many warnings about letting patterns of sin take control in our family. For example, we see the damage done by favoritism in the story of Isaac and later Jacob. There are dire consequences from the negligence of Eli, Samuel, and

David as their sons were allowed to do what was immoral and to show contempt for what was holy. Since the fathers didn't correct them, God did. Repeatedly, idolatry was the sin of many of Israel's kings that affected not only their families but also their nation. Thankfully, there are many resources available today, to help us with all such sins and consequences. I won't address them in this book but please remember, God is able and desires to set us free!

On a positive note, God told His people how to protect their families by training them to know His Word. Joshua 1:9 says, "This book of the law shall not depart from your mouth, but you shall meditate on it day and night, so that you may be careful to do according to all that is written in it; for then you will make your way prosperous and then you will have success."

In Deuteronomy 6:6-9, Moses instructs us to make this a part of our daily life.

> "These words which I am commanding you today shall be in your heart. And you shall teach them diligently to your sons and shall talk of them when you sit in your house and when you walk by the way and when you lie down and when you rise up. And you shall bind them as a sign on your hand ... and write them on the doorposts of your house and your gates."

In other words, studying, explaining and applying God's ways to your family will be the most effective way to confront sin in its early stages. Looking at our homes from God's perspective will help us see and correct any wrong attitudes and actions. Remember, these words and principles apply as much to us as parents as they do to our children. Let us learn together and humbly help each other yield to God's Word and Spirit. Let us intentionally add to our family's Treasure Box what the next generation will value and imitate. Be purposeful about leaving treasures of faith.

Chapter 2

STORIES FROM THE PAST

It seems appropriate to begin this conversation on heritage by looking at some of the ways past generations have enriched our current lives. Every culture, and every home, has its own collection of traditions and stories. It takes effort to maintain those traditions and to repeat them year after year. There may be times of financial need or physical exhaustion that require adjustments and a change in expectations. Yet, any investment in passing on something that builds community and honor is so worth it.

Some of the most precious memories we have as a family revolve around holidays and celebrations throughout the year. I am sure many of you have something you treasure about Christmas. It could be the special foods and smells of baking or dinner cooking and even the evergreen scent as the tree is set up in your home. Do you treasure the unique sounds of seasonal music and people talking and laughing together as they get to reconnect for what may be the only time each year? Encourage the retelling of your family's precious memories.

There are stories from the lives of our families that have shaped our understanding of history. For our family, there were stories from my dad during World War II. He was born into a family of eleven children, living on a farm in Norway. He has told numerous tales of those memorable days of occupation and war. We would sit by his feet, listening to all the details of his real-life adventures. We would be indignant at the confiscation of two of their homes and farms by German soldiers. We would be worried about the discovery of ammunition left behind, found by Dad and his friends. That they lived to tell their stories is in itself amazing.

Dad was often asked to tell "the pitchfork story" from the day of the occupation of Norway. From what I remember, the kids in their country school had been sent home because the adults knew something was about to happen. Dad, age nine, was out with a pitchfork doing his chores. He heard and saw the German planes flying over their farm, and he valiantly pointed his farm implement at them, as if wanting to defend his home and country. One fighter plane broke off from formation and circled back over their farm. The pilot might have thought someone was threatening his plane with a gun. He swooped down toward Dad, who realized he was in trouble. He had only one place to try to hide. He dove into the manure pile hoping his brown coveralls would be his camouflage. It must have worked because the plane rejoined his squadron and Dad lived to tell the tale. That story of bravery and a bit of childish folly will continue to be passed down through the years, instilling courage to defend what is right, for generations to come. There is also a new appreciation for the many in Norway who worked in the Resistance movement against Hitler and the Nazis.

I remember asking Dad if the children in the area were afraid of the German soldiers. He said most of the soldiers were just doing what they were ordered and actually treated them kindly. He said the soldiers were probably reminded of their own children back in Germany. They even shared pieces of candy with them, a rare treat in those days of war. The only ones they avoided were the Gestapo, who really were the brutal police. His stories added to a fuller appreciation of a difficult time in our family's history. (April 9, 1940)

As I said, my dad grew up on a farm in Norway. After the second World War, his dad, Kristian, would sail to New York City and work doing construction. This would supplement the income that came from subsistence farming that fed his family. The older children had to keep the farm running while he was gone. Every so often, my grandfather would return to Norway to work the farm again. He would eventually need to return to New York to earn the extra money his family still needed. As the children turned seventeen or eighteen years old, some of them would accompany him. They would begin to earn their own living. It is no surprise that self-sufficiency became an important value for these immigrant families. Quite a few of Dad's siblings spent some time in the United States. Many returned to Norway to raise their families.

Dad turned eighteen on the boat on his way to New York. He stayed and became a US citizen. He joined the Marines during the Korean War and made Brooklyn his home. He continued to work in Manhattan doing construction. We were a family of five children living as most did in those days with one source of income. With that said, our finances were sometimes stretched. Yet we had what we needed. We experienced for ourselves, that God provides.

Many families have experienced similar challenges due to war or oppression and have their own stories of honor and heroism, and often tragedy. Those events are threads in the tapestry of a culture and legacy that can unite and strengthen people and their descendants. The Bible says to "honor age." We need to take the time to invite those who are still with us, to tell us their stories. We need to appreciate the lessons learned and the burdens some of them bear in silence. Honoring the past is the foundation of preparing a legacy that will bless the ones who come behind.

I asked my husband's father, Grandpa Dave, to share a little about his own spiritual journey. This is part of what he wrote.

"My spiritual journey began in my mother's womb. Why do I say this? I say this because my parents were devout Christians, and when my mother knew she was pregnant with her fourth child, I am confident they began to pray for me. When I was just a few days old, my parents brought me to their church in Minneapolis, Minnesota, to be baptized. They knew that according to the Word of God, I 'was conceived in sin and born in iniquity' and thus needed God's grace from the moment I was born.

"My parents diligently had morning and evening devotions for my sisters and me, reading from the Bible and a classic children's Bible story book. They brought us to the midweek Bible study and prayer service on Wednesday evenings.

"When I was ten years old, I had what I would call a 'Law and Gospel' experience. As I listened to the Word being preached, I came under the conviction of sin. When my mother called me to come and eat lunch, I said I wasn't hungry. My mother then asked if I was sick? I said, 'No, but what is really bothering me is that I am such a big sinner.'"

"I will never forget the next thing she did and said. She came over to me, put her hands on my shoulders, and said with tears in her eyes, 'Oh David! I also am a bad sinner, just like you, and that's why God sent His Son into the world to die on the cross for sinners like you and me!' Then she prayed for me. I also prayed and asked Jesus to forgive my sins."

"I am now over ninety-four years old, and at the close of every day, I ask the Lord to forgive me my sins. I finish quoting 1 John 1:9 to myself, 'If we confess our sins, He is faithful and just to forgive our sins and to cleanse us from all our unrighteousness.' I can go to sleep and sleep soundly."

I know my husband's mom and dad continue to have a time reading the Bible together every day, followed by a time of prayer for their family and friends. They read through a monthly prayer letter from one of the many missionaries and pastors they know. Their faithfulness to pray is a powerful example to all of us. Anyone who has spent time in their home has a treasured memory of joining them around their large wood table for their time of prayer.

We planned a trip to Norway, the summer of 2020, for our fortieth anniversary. We had planned a stop to visit my father's only living sibling. I have many questions I wanted to ask, to get more of a sense of how faith was lived out in their home. The Covid-19 pandemic ended that travel opportunity. I do remember hearing about a great-grandmother who took in some kind of work. (I think it was sewing). I remember hearing that when someone came to pick up their finished work, she would often sit at the kitchen table and ask about her life and walk with God. I could imagine her asking. "So, how do you have it with the Lord?" a question my dad would often ask. Kitchen table evangelism was her ministry. I want to hear more about her. I want to hear more about my dad's mom and dad, and how they passed on a love for Jesus. I did not get to know them, since they lived in Norway. I do know they must have been people of faith, since many of my dad's siblings were faithful Christians.

I still hope someday to get answers about the faith journey of my dad, though his sister is now over ninety years old.

I asked my mom's sister, Lillian, about what she remembers about their dad. I can't ask my own mom since she died eight years ago. Lillian repeated what I often heard my mom say about their father.

"He was a wise man of few words. He had his Bible sitting on a small shelf near the kitchen table where he had time with His Lord. Our dad worked nights in a hotel in New York. He left for work at 4:00 p.m. and returned early the next morning. Our mom often waited up for him to return. I remember one time finding her baking cookies for Christmas at 1:00 a.m. while she waited."

I remember my own mom telling us as kids that her dad was a quiet man, who only spoke when he had something important to say. He chose his words wisely. We knew that if he started to speak, we were expected to stop and listen to what he said.

My mom talked about spending time lying next to her own mother, in the months before her fifth baby was due. Her mother had a heart condition and knew she would not survive childbirth. My grandmother knew she would not come home with her new baby. She took time with Mom, who was about twelve years old, to share what was on her heart. She wanted to prepare her as best as she could for the changes that were soon to come.

Tante Lillian said that in the midst of those days and months following their mom's death, their dad was a source of quietness and calm. She said she never experienced restlessness from him. He was a rock, a place of stability. One happy memory she had was when she was about seven or eight years old. As her dad prepared to leave for work, he would always say good-bye and then reach out to them with the handle of his umbrella.

He affectionately caught them around the neck, almost like a shepherd's staff. They knew he loved them.

Their father remarried a few years later. (His new wife was the one I knew as Bestemor. That is grandmother in Norwegian.) Where my grandfather was quiet, Bestemor was more of a communicator and planner. Lillian remembers hearing the manual typewriter clicking away, as she sat at her small desk, typing medical records for hospitals and doctors.. The money she earned was sent as financial support for a dear friend, a missionary in Africa named Anna Aandahl. I had never heard that connection between this missionary, for whom we prayed as a family, and my grandmother, till I asked about stories from the past. I do know Bestemor was faithful to serve and faithful to write letters to all the missionaries our church supported.

My parents have both gone to be with the Lord, so I asked some of my siblings to share some of their memories of our parents. My youngest sister shared some of her own memories, and some of the stories they told her. She added to the account of Mom's life after her mother died. Mom had to get her younger siblings ready for school in the morning. She did the laundry, ironing, and chores around the house. She also kept up with her own school work. "She was a hard-working, independent young woman." Mom told Helen that after her mom's funeral, she didn't want people to pity them for being motherless. She was determined to show that she could handle the responsibilities. The neighbors worried about her because she was always working. Mom said she didn't remember it being drudgery. She knew her dad appreciated all that she did and that made her happy. She did say that when her dad remarried, the responsibilities were lessened and she felt great relief. It was only then, that she realized how hard those years had been.

Mom always showed her love by serving. She taught us all kinds of life skills. I remember her teaching me how to rewire a lamp, among other helpful tasks. Helen commented that Mom raised us to be independent and to do our best. She was a good listener and valued our opinions. She told Helen that when we were teenagers, she chose to stay up late because she wanted to be available for those important conversations that would come up when we were ready to talk. Even when she was tired, she gave us her attention.

Mom would often sit in the living room reading her Bible. She said that reading God's promises gave her peace. Mom loved the Psalms because they were full of praise. She believed that we didn't praise God enough. Her love for the Word of God and her teaching that we should try to obey it in practical ways, molded my own love for the Bible. She taught and modeled what she believed.

You will hear other stories about my parents, but let me summarize the impact they made in the lives of their children and grandchildren. My brother David wrote this to be read at Dad's memorial service.

"Dad, I have a lot to be thankful for. You lived as an example of what it means to be a Godly man. As a parent, you were very supportive and active in my growth, encouraging me to participate to the best of my ability, to be patient, and to do what it takes to be a role model. As a husband, you took terrific care of Mom. We know you loved the Lord and that you shared that with almost everyone you encountered."

I see threads of how these lives are woven into the tapestry of our family heritage. A passion for God's Word, a passion for souls, a servant's heart in ministry, and a sacrificial investment in their children and grandchildren are all treasures that have been deposited in the Family Treasure Box. This is not an inheritance of financial wealth, but we are rich in treasures of faith. In view of their example, I want to be purposeful to add to the legacy of faith. I want to teach my children to honor the faithfulness of those who have gone before us. I want them to see that "faith comes from hearing and hearing by the Word of God." (Romans 10:17) Take the time to do an inventory of your own family's examples of faith. Be purposeful in finding ways to make those stories part of your family identity. We can learn from the good times and the hard times, that God was faithful in the past and is still faithful today.

Chapter 3
A Passion For Missions

I wonder if being a family and community of immigrants contributed to our family having an interest in missions around the world. My husband's grandmother came to the United States from Norway and eventually ended up in the Midwest at a small Bible School. She became concerned about people in Asia needing to hear about the hope of forgiveness through Jesus' work on the cross. She finished school in Minnesota and took off for Seattle, Washington. Her desire was to take a ship to go overseas to be a missionary. Unfortunately, by the time she reached Seattle, the financing for her trip was no longer available. She stayed in the Seattle area and married another Norwegian. Together they started a church in their home. The congregation became a faithful supporter of missionaries and the starting place of several other congregations on the west coast.

Her daughter, my mother-in-law, married a man who also had a heart for missions. They spent time in Japan, with her husband, Dave, teaching in a seminary which trained Japanese pastors. Upon return to the United States, they served multiple congregations which were faithful to send, and to pray for those who could go as missionaries. My father-in-law served on the world mission board for our denomination for thirty years. Their son, Joel, and his wife, Liz, ended up in an Asian country teaching and sharing God's message of hope. They, in turn, were able to encourage their coworkers and together with national Christians, were faithful witnesses to the love of the one true God.

Currently, many of the grandchildren have found ways to serve in a variety of ministries, some overseas and others here in the United States. There are those that are using their skills and talents to do ministry in the arena of sports. Some have helped in church ministries with technology assistance, music ministry, youth work, and teaching. Many have also shared in ministries of prayer, encouragement, and even giving of their financial resources. God is the one who gives us our individual abilities and He has the plan for how He will use them.

My own parents used their home to serve many missionary families whenever they came back on furlough. Their children became our friends and their world did not seem very far away. I loved going with my parents to the airport to say good-bye to these people who were now family. We watched as they piled their luggage at the ticket counter and prepared to go back to the work God had put in their hearts to do. How much easier it was to pray for them because we knew them better. We learned to care about the people they loved, who needed to hear that God loved them. These childhood experiences actually prepared me for the good-byes I would one day have to make myself. I have also had to stand at the ticket counter with piles of luggage, as my own kids answer God's call to go. Their world seems not so far away, and I know God is also going with them.

I often remember sitting at my parents' dining room table listening to the stories of life and ministry from many servants of God. One missionary heard that I was studying French and hoping to someday be a missionary. He spoke only French to me during that entire evening. My lack of fluency was a humbling experience. It made me realize how much I still had to learn! By the age of thirteen, I knew in my heart that God wanted me to be willing to go to Africa. I spent six years studying French and started college as a linguistics major. I was willing and preparing to go wherever God would lead.

Though I was expecting to go myself, God had other plans. He used my years of training to equip me for a different set of ministries. He also prepared me to be ready to send my own children, should God ask it of them. God wastes nothing! Now our oldest daughter, her husband, and family are sharing the hope of salvation with the people of Cambodia. Another daughter and her husband have served as nurses for several tours on the Mercy Ship off the coast of Africa. Now, our youngest is preparing to share the Gospel somewhere overseas. She has studied French, Chinese, and now Arabic to be prepared for whatever God may ask. In the meantime, she is involved in church and campus ministries to international students here in the United States. What a joy to hear each time one of her friends comes to faith in Jesus!

It is evident that the passions and interests of one generation can greatly affect the direction of the next. I remember a lady speaking to us about support for missions. She said the financial support was so welcome and necessary. Then she challenged us to consider whether we would be willing to also give the treasure of our children and grandchildren to be part of God's work around the world. What an important challenge to consider! We mustn't discourage our kids from doing whatever it is God asks. Some are asked to go. Some are asked to give. All are asked to pray. We are all a part of God's plan and mission.

Take a few minutes to look at the talents and interests of your own family. Is there a passion and aptitude for sports? Your children and grandchildren will most likely find encouragement to test their skills in that arena. There is an open door right now to be a witness through coaching and playing. Does your family have a special giftedness in music? Your children will need to have the commitment necessary to excel. Encourage them in their early years to share their ministry of music in a nursing home or church service. They can find a safe, attentive audience with people who will love and encourage them. Do you as parents have the skills needed to build a business? Your children will have an inside look at the investment and sacrifice it takes to succeed. They will have an advantage in starting their own businesses since they will also know some of the pitfalls to avoid and the resources they will require. They may become the next generation of financial supporters for the work God will do in their generation. God can use anyone who is available to Him. He will use all our talents for what will certainly have value into eternity.

What an opportunity we have today to look back at the generations that came before us. We can learn how they lived and what they valued. We need to know how God worked through them. The older generations in our family rarely told anyone about their giving and sacrifice. They took seriously the admonition to "not let the right hand know what the left hand is doing when you give, and the God who sees what is done in secret will repay." (Matthew 6:3) That secrecy was well-intentioned, but many in the next generations may never know about this "call to give" that was so powerful. At some point, those stories need to be told for the Glory of God.

My one son wanted to get his grandfather (Hans) on video telling the many stories of his life, in his own enthusiastic and entertaining way. Unfortunately, we waited too long and those videos never got recorded. Take your opportunity now while you have it. Record for the generations to come, the many ways God has blessed your family.

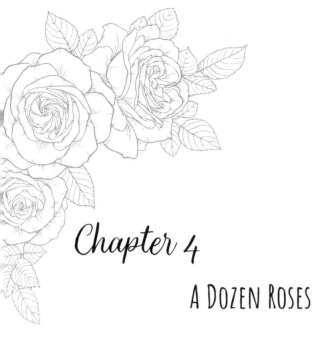

Chapter 4

A Dozen Roses

My dad was an incurable romantic. We all knew he treasured my mom. He would often put candles on the table for breakfast with her, before he left for work at 4:30 a.m. He loved to bring her flowers when he could afford it. There was a flower stand on the way home right at his exit off the highway. There were times when there just wasn't money for that gift of love. I can't tell you how often I heard him say to her, "I bought you a dozen roses … in my heart!" That became just as real an act of love as the actual flowers on the table.

My husband and I have also lived most of our married life on one income. We decided that homeschooling was the right choice for educating our children, which meant I stayed home to teach. There have been times when just basic needs had to be put on a priority prayer list. Even now when I would love to buy something for someone, but can't afford it, I will take a picture or screenshot of it and send the image with the message, "I bought this for you today in my heart." Everyone smiles, knowing the sentiment came from me but also from my dad.

We have learned to ask the question, "Is this a need or a want?" We will pray and wait till God provides the actual item, or a way to earn it. That means budgeting for food and clothing and any other other extras. When our kids were younger, we would tell them what we could afford, and if they wanted a higher-priced item, they had to earn and save their money to pay for it. For example, the boys were good basketball players and often did paper routes to be able to get better quality basketball shoes. They also had to save to buy a bicycle or help pay half the cost to go to a week-long summer Bible camp.

You might think they complained about the work, especially since we lived in Minnesota and North Dakota at the time. Those paper routes had to be done seven days a week all year long. There was no excuse to not get it done. They learned how to work. They learned the value of labor. They took better care of their bikes and shoes and enjoyed their special outings because they had worked to make it happen. They also had lots of work experience by the time they finished high school.

Something else my dad modeled was the joy of giving! My dad loved to give gifts even if it was "a dollar." He always had some cash in his wallet and he looked for ways to "give it away." It brought him joy. The Bible says, in Romans 12:8, that "he who gives, should give with liberality." Dad loved to bless people and that included his kids and grandkids. He would ask a little grandchild, "Could you take this comb and comb my hair?" He could do it himself even though one elbow had been destroyed by a fall from a defective ladder at work. He had no ability to bend that arm. But this request was not due to his arm; he just wanted to have an excuse to hand her "a dollar." He gave "a dollar" to each Sunday School boy in his class for every Bible verse he memorized. I know Dad considered that an eternal investment, not a bribe.

He believed in the value of work but also in the blessing of sharing. He and Mom taught us to find joy in giving, even more than receiving. Every year as part of our Christmas celebration, they would take us to a local Woolworth Store (similar to Walmart). We would be given "a dollar" each to buy gifts for our family. We all shopped at the same time considering our options and thinking about what would bring delight to our siblings and parents. One dollar bought more than it does today but we still needed to budget that money. We spent time collaborating with each other if we found something we couldn't afford to buy alone. Then when we got home, Mom put wrapping paper, scissors, and tape on the table and we wrapped all our gifts at the same time, at the same table. It was a game to wrap so no one saw the gift they were getting.

We tried to keep that joy of giving and blessing each other as part of our own family's celebration. Our seven kids started with $5 apiece to shop for Christmas. That increased over time. As they were older and able to work, they could add their own money to their resources. Even today, we have tried to figure out how to simplify this process, since there are now seven children, five spouses, and thirteen grandchildren. There needs to be a sensitivity to individual family finances and budgets. But no one wants to stop having the chance to think and plan and choose a way to bless family members. Since we are scattered all over the world, our time together is often only once a year. We look forward to time together, and to the fun of giving a blessing.

One year, the oldest of our children was in college. She had run out of money to pay for her tuition. The girls that were home found all kinds of ways to earn some money, even cleaning the church. They wanted to earn what Becky needed so she could take her finals. Other siblings sent in what they could give. What a joy it was to watch them give her what they had worked so hard to provide!

Another year, Sarah. the youngest, wanted to learn how to play guitar. She didn't know it but her brothers and sisters pooled their money to buy one for her. Her oldest brother had a friend who played guitar who helped to pick one out. You can imagine the surprise and gratefulness that was expressed and the love that was shared between those kids.

This thoughtfulness has shown up in so many fun ways throughout the years, as the kids have gotten older. One particular gift was sent to Mary who turned eighteen while away at college. She was far from any family member who could celebrate with her. One sister-in-law made a picture show with her little girl who was less than one year old. She dressed Savannah in eighteen outfits, holding a letter in each picture that together, spelled "HAPPY BIRTHDAY, MARY!" Think of the time and effort that went into making this gift. Mary certainly knew she was remembered.

A few years ago, Sarah, our youngest, spent her summer in France studying French. The rest of the kids collaborated in buying me a plane ticket to spend a week with her in France. I met her in Paris for the weekend, and spent the rest of the week in Bordeaux where she was living. That was my Mother's Day gift. It was such a blessing to me, and to Sarah, to share that time. Even as I consider her doing missions overseas, I have peace that she knows how to navigate a new culture and place. I have seen her do it.

I have also watched Jon provide work for Dave, his younger brother. Dave lived at his house in Minnesota in the first summers after high school. Jon bought David his first good camera, which was the beginning of a passion and business for him. Recently, David and his wife, Armine, checked in on Rachel when she spent a few weeks in Los Angeles for an Opera Program. Though they lived hours north in California, they made sure she had food to cook in the university dorm, and a place to go for a break.

Our fifth child, Mary, finds joy in planning events that let her spend intentional time with her siblings. She has lived during the last few years, within driving distance of her younger two sisters who were away in college. One fall, when Rachel was settling into her semester classes, Mary went to visit her at school. Mary noticed Rachel's planner on the desk. While she waited for her to return from class, she opened the book and to her dismay, the planner was empty. Mary took each syllabus and entered the dates of major tests and due dates for projects, for each class that semester. Rachel was so grateful, since she just didn't find time to do the organizing. The sisters have gone hiking, rock climbing, running 10 K races, or out for coffee. It is fun to see them making memories together!

Liz hired Rachel to watch her three-year-old when Rachel moved north after grad school. That access to New York City allowed Rachel to find a teacher and coach for the next step in her training. The income was a big provision for Rachel to help fund those lessons. Having her sister care for her little one was a major blessing for Liz. I could tell story after story of ways the kids, now adults, continue to bless each other. Their giving has brought joy to my heart!

What an investment to teach children to love to give, as opposed to looking to receive! God is always reminding us to show love to one another. This should start in the home and continue to influence all of life. I am thankful for that mindset being passed on to us in our early years of life. Live with the joy of giving!

Chapter 5

RICE AND REDEMPTION

There once was a grandmother who had her granddaughter helping her in the kitchen. They were working on preparing dinner, which included a side of cooked rice. Unfortunately, the bowl containing the uncooked rice tipped and the rice fell to the floor. The young girl watched her grandmother kneel on the floor and pick up all the rice, piece by piece. Grandma carefully washed the rice, one grain at a time, so it could be reused.

The little girl asked, "Grandma, can't you just sweep it up and throw it away. You could just start over with new rice?"

Grandma smiled and answered her, "Yes, I could. That would be easier. But I like to be reminded that God treats you and me and all people the same way. He reaches down to pick us up, one by one, since we are unclean from our sin. He washes each of us so we can be usable for His purposes. He could have swept away all of mankind when they sinned in the Garden of Eden. He could have started over with new creations. But He has a plan to show us that He loves us and is able to cleanse us from all our sin. I am thanking Him for His love for me as I wash these pieces of rice."

Following His action of forgiveness which cleanses us from sin, God begins to change the heart and mind to prepare us for the "good works which He prepared beforehand that we should walk in them." (Ephesians 2:10) We usually think about those good works as what is done by ministries through the church and through nonprofits and parachurch organizations. We need to look deeper at the individual plan God has. We are each created with unique talents and given individual gifts to encourage the body of believers.

Sometimes we can serve as individual family groups, which allows us to benefit from sharing resources, motivation and vision. For our family with seven unique children, we have tried to model being part of the body of believers in the local church. We have been intentional to discover the individual gifts God has given, in preparation for the adult ministries they would eventually have. The church and the family can be built-in cheering squads provided by God. What a treasure to have had a loving source of "adopted grandparents" who added their mentoring and prayer support for our roaming children who often live far from their own grandparents.

Our job as parents is to pray and to encourage. My favorite verse in this endeavor is from Psalm 5:3. "In the morning, O Lord, you will hear my voice. In the morning, I will order my prayer to You and eagerly watch." Please allow me to model how that happens with our family. My hope is that you will be prompted to look at the special ways God has invested in your family.

One by one, God allows us to discern the interests and capabilities that need to be nurtured and enabled. Becky, the oldest, has a heart for those who don't know Jesus. Even as a child, she seemed to see the person who was standing alone or seemed uncomfortable. Her vision was to be involved in international missions. When she was eight years old, she wrote a song about telling "your friends and your neighbors and those across the sea of the hope that only comes from Calvary." Beginning in her teens, she did children's ministries and evangelism in Hungary, watched missionary children in Singapore (while the parents did pre-field training), taught English to students in China, and worked with many international students during her years in college. Now she serves with her husband and children in Cambodia, a place where there is a great need to bring God's message of hope.

One of her spiritual gifts is helps. She would do anything someone asked in order to come alongside and serve. If you needed a teacher, she would teach. If you needed childcare, she would work in the nursery. If you needed rides, she would help drive people where they needed to go. She also had a sensitivity to stand up for what is right and true according to the Scriptures, even if it meant standing alone.

Jon, our second child, is a natural leader. Even when he was seven years old, the neighbor boys wanted to do whatever he did. They called him "The King." Every time we moved to a new community and church, he would rise to positions of leadership. Interestingly, God would require him to start at the bottom, over and over. Maybe the Lord had some specific character qualities He wanted to develop. I am sure that was not always fun for him. Yet God knew the best way to reach his heart. Jon was always pretty clear about right and wrong and saw issues as more black and white than gray. I always thought he would make a great juvenile judge. That was not the direction God led him. Jon had a full ride engineering scholarship, but quit college to start a business which he still runs today. Even as a busy father and businessman, he has spent time studying and discussing theological truths. I am glad he has the desire to know what God has to say about many, many issues and to passionately pursue understanding.

One of his other gifts is the spiritual gift of giving. From the time Jon was young, he spent time and any hard-earned paper route money trying to bless his parents and siblings. He would start in September looking through Lego catalogues, choosing Christmas gifts for his brothers and sisters. To this day, Jon has a desire to bless where God prompts with the resources God has given him.

Elizabeth was one of our very social children. She seemed to understand from as young as three, that people needed prayer or some other kind of help. She would come home from church and say, "We need to pray for 'so and so' because ..." That discernment and compassion are tools God uses even to this day, as she finds ways to bless our family. One year, Liz had each of us do a StrengthsFinder survey. We spent time together going through the results. We became more

conscious of how each of us fits into the dynamics of decision-making and communication. The spouses of those that were married also joined in on the survey, identifying their additional contributions to the family.

Liz has worked as a business consultant, especially in transferring a business from one generation to another. I am sure God continues to use her skills and gifts to bring perspective to the family members of the businesses she serves. She tries to help them agree on a family vision and set of priorities in order to move forward in unity. Their gracious support of ministries around the world could be lost if the businesses liquidate and close up due to division.

If you asked her siblings what one word to link to Liz, it might be "systems." For any event that needs organizing or planning, Liz can make a spreadsheet to make a gathering go smoothly. There are guides for Christmas gift giving, meal planning for family reunions, wedding responsibilities and schedules so nothing gets missed. She has sensed that I don't take charge of family events like I used to. I have started to step back in a room filled with adult planners and decision makers. But then, who is in charge? That void can cause confusion and poor communication. It can also cause conflict. Liz has become a proactive initiator to help our gatherings be as stress free and happy as possible. I am still trying to figure out how to navigate the world of all adult "children."

David is a creative spark in family gatherings. He usually has a new addition to our family meal plan. He also provides the newest tech to help us be more effective in what we are doing. He challenges me to try a new software or app to make my job easier but then makes me figure it out for myself. He is always available with a solution if I am desperate. I so appreciate his willingness to help his musical sister as she begins to build a website and a music business. He has probably already researched every camera, microphone, and tool she might need to do auditions and recordings in this time of virtual gatherings. He is technologically fearless. He has found those skills to be a way to help his church go online and reach the people of their congregation while the state keeps them from meeting in person.

Hospitality is also at the heart of David's life. From the time he was little, David would be the first one to run to the kitchen to put some cookies or treats on a plate to serve anyone who came to our door. As an adult, he would love to have people come over to his home and make them feel welcome. That was always one of the character qualities that helped him in his photography business. People felt comfortable around him. He is quick to say yes to help and serve.

Mary is the oldest of the younger three girls. She was often in charge of supervising them during the school hours for the older children, or during church Bible studies being held in our home. She became really good at telling stories and keeping the younger girls busy. Mary is a natural teacher. Anything I taught her, she taught the younger girls. If it was folding towels or laundry, she had them help her by making it a game. Mary became the storyteller for our long-distance car trips. We as adults were just as captivated as the children, waiting to hear what would happen next.

Mary has a compassionate heart. She is a pediatric intensive-care nurse, and with her husband (cardiac intensive care RN), spent several sessions on the Mercy Ship off the coast of Africa. She knows how to make a difference. Mary also takes friendship seriously. She is intentional about meeting with someone to encourage them or pray with them. For example, when she was living in Florida after college, she signed up to visit an older lady in a nursing home and would often go to play Scrabble with her. She hosted a small group Bible study while attending a new church being planted in her area, and did their children's ministry on Sunday mornings. She was willing to help wherever needed.

Rachel is our comedian and singer. Her sense of humor is a gift to our family. She is a lot like my dad's sisters who were just fun ladies who always made us feel loved. Also, from the time Rachel was three, I believe she thought she was Shirley Temple. She is always ready to sing when asked, to bring a song of comfort or praise or hope. She takes the leading of the Spirit seriously as she prepares music for a concert or a service. So many people have been encouraged through her ministry. She is sensitive to the needs of the people around her, and her mercy is so often directed to them.

Sarah has benefited from watching all her siblings who have gone ahead of her, learning from their mistakes and gaining from their steps of faith. She has a quiet ministry to people who don't yet know Jesus. She has worked with international students through English language classes and also through intentional time set aside for one-on-one meetings with friends from school or church. She is willing to serve, like making food for an international student meeting or playing piano or guitar for a senior citizen nursing home. She is praying about missions in the near future, having studied French, Chinese, a little Spanish, and now Arabic.

Why did I go through this list? I want to encourage you as parents and grandparents to look for the ways your children/grandchildren are especially gifted or passionate. Their interests may change over time, but they need guidance, resources, and encouragement to be free to test their unique skills and passions. Freedom to fail is important if they are going to be able to live with courage and not with fear.

I believe we have to look at our children the way God does. Each individual has value to Him and to us as parents. The world tends to look at children as a collective, as if one size discipline and one size education fits all. No matter how you tend to provide for the education of your kids, they still need a challenge and assistance. Let me share one decision, which allowed us to give that individualized attention to our kids and which ultimately made our many moves less traumatic for them.

We chose to homeschool our children, starting when the oldest was almost five years old. She was so ready to learn to read but she missed the cutoff date for enrollment in kindergarten by a few weeks. I called a friend who had been a public-school teacher but had decided to teach her daughter at home. I looked at what she was using to teach and thought, "*I can do this.*" The focus was on teaching foundational learning skills and giving your child a love of learning. I decided to give it a try. I could always change our plans for first grade. So year after year, child by child, we evaluated their progress using the same standardized tests the public schools used. A one-year trial lasted for twenty-seven years as my seven children finished high school. There were individual opportunities to experience a classroom setting at a public elementary school, two Christian high schools, one in Minnesota where five of the seven received their high school diplomas, and a public high school. All arrangements were chosen for specific children for a specific time period or class.

We moved seven times over those years, serving churches from coast to coast. God knew that our homeschooling would make those transitions easier, at least educationally. In hindsight, this was the right decision for our family. I don't think this works for everyone. No one should feel pressured to make educating at home their family's choice. I believe God leads parents to find His best for their children. I have to say, I loved every minute of our journey.

I would love to offer a few blessings that came from school at home. My children learned to know each other well and had the chance to invest in each other without age-graded limitations. I could include them in all kinds of ministries that happened during the day, like going to nursing homes to sing or read or just greet the elderly people they met. They were able to learn ministry skills like puppetry and drama, working with the little ones in the nursery, and being part of many hospitality opportunities. They were very comfortable relating to people of all ages.

As I have described in this chapter, my children have a variety of interests and aptitudes, which allowed me to encourage them to excel in their strengths. It also allowed me to spend one-on-one time when there was an area of struggle. They really had one-on-one tutoring for the subjects that needed it and a one room schoolhouse experience for things like history and science, and sometimes literature.

This choice has contributed to a family identity that binds us together in a special way.

Every family will have their own experiences that unite. It might be over music or sports or business experiences or even participation in the life of a congregation. One of my friends has been intentional to call her family together to share in a family legacy day. They talk about what God has done in the year just passed and decide together how to use their family resources to support ministries or causes in the year ahead. They plan family vacations to build a treasury of memories This helps their children and now their spouses and a growing number of grand-children, celebrate their family identity. We can fall into these kinds of opportunities or we can be intentional to plan them. It is what we do in the here and now that makes our hopes for the next generation possible.

After the 2020 shutdown of most school systems, due to a highly contagious virus, many parents were forced to become the teachers for their children. For some, this became a welcome opportunity to spend quality time with their kids. This could have been an opportunity for these students to focus on their personal areas of expertise or passion. For others, there was a stress that came from the sudden need to be current in the new methods being used to teach math or science or language skills. This was particularly difficult for those with older children. I am sure there will be stories told for years to come about the unique individual experiences of both parents and kids. I hope the memories will be filled with courage and, probably in hindsight, a good dose of laughter.

There is a verse from Proverbs 27:23 talking to shepherds about their sheep. "Know well the condition of your flocks, and pay attention to your herds." I think this pertains to parents and children as well. We only have a short time to invest in the lives of our kids. It can be so much fun to see them thrive in the "good works," which God has prepared for them.

Chapter 6

One-To-One Mentoring

*E*ncouraging our children to be effective as uniquely gifted people is only one way this individualized approach to child-rearing is applied. We found that discipline and character training also require a knowledge of how each individual responds to teaching and correction. Unrealistic expectations usually cause discouragement, so think small steps and patient teaching.

I first learned to ask if a child's behavior was due to childishness or foolishness. What is the difference? Childishness is the result of immaturity or incomplete teaching and training. If I made a demand that was not obeyed fully, I had to ask if I had trained that child as I should. For example, if I told a child to clean his room before going out to play or watching a TV show and it was only done part way, was his incomplete job willful disobedience? Does that child know what I expect or am I assuming he knows?

My mom used to tell me to make obedience easy. For example, every child was expected to make his bed before going to school or doing other activities. She purposefully chose bedspreads for my brothers' room that would make it easy for them to fix their bunk beds neatly. She bought comforters that didn't need to be tucked under a pillow and also had a seam or visible line to help them see when it was hanging evenly on each side. It was easy for them to see if they had met her standard for making their beds.

I remember hearing a military man sharing at a high school graduation that the very act of making a bed each morning gives you your first accomplishment of the day. The Bible warns against loving sleep, since it leads to laziness. Proverbs 6:6–11 says to go to the ant and see how she prepares and works for the future. "How long will you lie down, O sluggard? When will you arise from your sleep? A little sleep, a little slumber, a little folding of the hands to rest. Your poverty will come in like a vagabond and your need like an armed man." Sleep is important but not more than you need, and making that bed signals your mind to move on to something productive.

If cleaning a room was done poorly, I needed to stop and make sure that each child knew what I expected and how to accomplish it. I can give a small child a daily chart with a picture of a neatly made bed, a picture of folded clothes and toys put away in a basket. I can work to help him do it correctly and praise his efforts. Once I see the task is done as I taught, I can assign it as his responsibility. Anything less than the standard is either laziness or disobedience. We can call that foolishness. Childishness needs continued training. Foolishness needs correction.

We can make training fun for our children. My kids would run and ask me if I knew where their book or toy or lost shoe was. I would ask if they had looked for it themselves. Usually they would answer yes. I would ask, "Did you really look with your eyes?" They knew what that meant. I had played a game of hiding something for them to find. I usually put it where they had to physically get on their knees or move something to find it. Many times, I had seen their lost item in my travels around the house, so I would direct them to a specific room and prompt them to keep looking. Not wanting to frustrate them, I would go with them and, if necessary, show them where the item was. Eventually, the kids got good at finding things for themselves.

Our job as parents is to teach what we expect, or more importantly, what God expects. The Bible says, "Woe to those who call good, evil and evil, good." God wants our children to love what is right in His eyes, because they love Him. They need to reject what is evil in His eyes because He loves them and wants to protect them. We want our children to love to do right just because it is right.

This takes intentionality and time. To do this inconsistently is to lead our children into confusion or foolishness. Foolishness is knowing what to do but not doing it, or knowing what NOT to do and doing it anyway. Doing wrong is part of this, but so is not doing what is right. Knowing what love should lead us to do and say, as God directs, is important to explain.

The Bible talks about foolishness being bound up in the heart of a child and the rod of correction removing it. Before the rod of correction can be applied, there must be teaching. I am not advocating corporal punishment for every infraction, for that would be lazy correction. Save a spanking for deliberate, willful rebellion, usually in the first few years, especially when that disobedience could result in injury. A child who runs to cross the street must learn to wait. Yes, teach and hold her hand and warn of danger. If that child is determined to run anyway, we should love them enough to make that kind of rebellion stop. She needs to know that tone of voice that means STOP—DANGER. This is so much easier when a child is young.

A spanking may be needed but **NEVER** in a moment of anger and **NEVER** more than a quick "PAY ATTENTION!" A spanking is **NEVER** meant as punishment, but rather as a warning that the child's behavior is imminently dangerous. A two-year-old doesn't usually have the verbal ability to reason and bring his will under conscious control, but you can't wait till he understands the danger, to demand obedience. Think about a child running into a street, or touching an electrical outlet or something that is hot. Be attentive to what fascinates him and teach "No", consistently. Encourage with positive words and hugs for quick obedience.

"Everyone must be quick to hear, slow to speak, and slow to anger, for the anger of man does not achieve the righteousness of God." (James 1:19–20)

Isn't this the goal, that our children would learn to love what is right and good in God's eyes? My anger as a parent won't accomplish that result. Usually anger comes from repeatedly allowing disobedience and rebellion to happen without correction, often because we want to show mercy. Truthfully, sometimes we are just too tired to be consistent. Unfortunately, we often teach our children that their poor choices are not serious enough to be confronted. They begin to expect that they can get away with doing what they want. They usually know when we have reached our limit of patience and mercy. That tone of voice or look on your face will alert them to the need to finally yield. Withholding correction is actually training them to disobey. Remember, too, that the older the child becomes, the more serious the consequences will be in the life of a soon-to-be adult. There are many ways to compel obedience. Be creative in the consequences you choose to apply. If possible, connect the disobedience to the consequence. For example, if a child leaves his bike in the driveway, restrict the use of the bike for a period of time. He will get the connection.

Here is the standard for obedience that I heard in a child-discipline course called <u>Growing Kids God's Way</u> (by Gary and Anne Marie Ezzo). "Obedience must be immediate, complete, without challenge, and without complaint." This is pretty sobering because that is the same standard God requires of everyone – including parents. A parent's hurt pride, and embarrassment should never be the foundation of correction. Restoring a broken relationship should always be the goal. Sin has broken the relationship with God, and He has offered restoration. If we confess and repent, He will forgive. People who are hurt may not quickly forgive, but we should teach what it means to confess and repent and even make restitution. Hopefully we will find healing for the relationships we have damaged. This takes love, humility, and wisdom.

We need to be prepared with a planned response to disobedience. What consequences are you committed to carry out? Don't threaten what you are unwilling to finish. Know what works for each child. For example, some of my children would love to be sent to their room. They loved to have a chance to play alone or read a book. That was not an effective consequence for them. For other children who loved social interaction, isolation was the perfect consequence. I would explain they couldn't return to the fun until they had "confessed" their wrongdoing and until there was reconciliation with a parent, with God, and with any offended child. "I'm sorry" is not enough. That statement may just be feeling sorry for their consequences, or for just being caught. Teach them to say, "I know I was wrong when I _____. Would you forgive me for (hurting, disobeying, etc.) you?" Those acknowledgements take humility and repentance.

Forgiveness should then be quick and their humility rewarded with a hug or words of reconciliation.

Don't rush the work of the Holy Spirit in the heart of a child. If there really isn't humility or repentance, the child won't sense the relief and healing that comes from being forgiven. Was the behavior breaking God's moral rules? Was the behavior breaking family rules? Be ready to use God's words if possible, to explain what you are correcting. The Holy Spirit uses God's Word to prick the conscience. He also warns us of impending sin or gives encouragement when we choose what is right.

The Ten Commandments, explained in a child-friendly way, and the Fruits of the Spirit from Galatians 5:22–23 are your tools for parenting. Ask, "Was that action patient? Was your behavior kind?" etc. Be forewarned that the Holy Spirit is often working on us as parents using the same standards. It may be that your child's disobedience is what God will use to confront your own impatience. Remember God is training us as His children. At the same time, He is holding us accountable to train the children He puts under our care.

Chapter 7

Don't Rush The Fruit

This is clearly an agricultural principle. If we know something is growing in our garden and watch it day after day, we can get impatient to pick it and taste it. I know seeing strawberry fields in late May makes me impatient to pick a few quarts and rush home to make homemade freezer jam. If I pick too early, those berries won't have the taste needed to provide the delicious treat my family loves, especially in the months of winter.

This concept applies to character development as well. As we teach and train our children, or disciple new believers, we can begin to see the work of the Holy Spirit and get excited. Our expectations may lead us to put someone in a place of responsibility that they are not prepared to handle. How often don't we see someone's emerging gifts and, with enthusiasm, invite them to lead a department in our business or ministry in our church. Unless we provide an experienced team member to help someone navigate the new challenges, the willing worker often quits. This poor experience can lead to embarrassment or discouragement. The next request to serve may be met with "No, thank you."

My mom used to say we need to teach precept upon precept. In order words, there is so much foundational teaching that must happen before we introduce more complex principles. I think we are more careful to take time for step-by-step teaching for those who are young in age. It is not easy to know how to proceed when the new believer is a mature, competent adult. If they have a background in the Scriptures, the process can be faster. We have to be more intentional to get to know the new believers who are being welcomed into fellowship and ministry.We are too quick to assume someone knows what is required to step into leadership. We are quick to appoint and move on. We need to be team members as a person "grows" into opportunities for ministry.

There are so many examples in the Bible of people who had a calling in their lives but were not given the positions they expected right away. Joseph had a dream about a future leadership position but went through slavery in Egypt, wrongful accusations and time in jail, and finally a management role under Pharaoh. All his experience prepared him to do what God had planned for his life.

Moses was another man who knew God had spared him for some role in helping his people. Even with all the training in the courts of Egypt, God wanted him to understand the challenges of living in the wilderness and leading sheep. When ready, God allowed him to lead the Israelites through that same wilderness, acting as the commander of the military and national judge and lawmaker. It took eighty years for his preparation. He was ready in God's timing.

David, the future king of Israel, had been anointed as a youth to take over the throne, after the death of King Saul. There were many areas of training this shepherd would need before being king. There were multiple times David could have ended Saul's life, even under the excuse of self-defense. It would have given him the position right away. David said he wouldn't act against God's anointed because he trusted the timing of the Lord. In the meantime, David learned how to lead an army, how to seek the Lord's will for his actions, and even how his failures could cause suffering for his people. His choices had consequences. He was not perfect, but he led his people to worship and seek their God.

I like to think that God has individualized education plans for spiritual growth. Every child of His needs to first learn how to respond to His authority as their Father. They need to find security in His promise "to never leave them nor forsake them." They need to grow in their experience of His compassion and mercy. They also need to be taught to talk with Him, through learning to pray and worship. Young Christians, like young children, need to learn how to feed themselves. This is the stage when a new believer spends guided time in God's Word, with the help of a person who has studied the Bible . There are always questions that need answers from other parts of the Scripture. How quickly these things are learned, depends on the individual journey of each "spiritual child."

A young believer is not only one who is young in physical years. A person in their sixties can be a young Christian who needs to grow in her relationship with the Father. To be truthful, I sometimes think we never stop acting like children, especially in times of confusion and stress. We struggle with slow progress and often get discouraged when we don't see the changes we anticipate for ourselves. Sometimes we are impatient with spiritual growth in people in our families or church. Please remember, God loves the "little ones" and knows their weaknesses. He doesn't give up on any of us.

As a spiritual child matures, she becomes like an elementary aged child. She is hungry to learn and eager to help. This is the age when we tend to invite a person to step in to serve, often because we love their enthusiasm. This is a great time to train and give experience in ministry. Be careful to make this more of an apprenticeship arrangement. If we fail to offer supervision and support, a "child" may get discouraged by failing at a task that requires more training or maturity. I have seen many capable people step in and out of serving because they were not protected from criticism because of mistakes that could have been avoided.

Allow me to give you a hypothetical example. A capable mature person begins to attend a church and quickly wants to find a way to join in ministry and congregational life. She hears about the need for a Bible study coordinator. She had the skills needed to do such a job. Since no one else volunteered, she was invited to be in charge. The Bible Study ministry's organization and structure became much more efficient, and communication with participants was so helpful. As the summer drew to a close, it was time to pick the curriculum for the upcoming fall studies. Our gracious coordinator looked up popular studies on the internet and picked the top three for her groups. She ordered books and leadership guides.

As the fall began, questions about the theology and biblical interpretation began to be voiced. There began to be an undercurrent of discontent and criticism. The concerns went to the pastor and elders. When they asked her about her choices, she felt discouraged by the criticism and gave up her position. What went wrong? This person was not an immature adult nor an unqualified leader. Her management skills were excellent. She was unfamiliar with the process needed to vet the teaching materials for the church (and really for most churches). Had there been someone who mentored her in this role, she would have learned how to look at a curriculum and what doctrinal issues might cause dissension. She should have been informed that it is always wise to send teaching materials, as well as suggestions for the teachers she wanted to use, to the Elder Board. They could add their discernment to the process. That would have provided cover for her should there be any difficulties. Instead, a potentially well-qualified leader was lost.

How does the Bible define spiritual maturity? The writer of Hebrews recognized that some people in the early church who ought to have been teachers, still needed someone to teach them the basics. He called that kind of teaching "milk." (See Hebrews 6:1–2 for a fuller description.)

"... solid food is for the mature, who because of practice have their senses trained to discern good and evil." (Hebrews 5:14)

It is time spent in God's Word and practice looking at issues through God's teaching on good and evil, that leads a person to spiritual maturity. Please remember that no one arrives at this fully while still living here on earth. Even at this stage of growth, we cannot rush the fruit of God's work in any individual life. God uses His Word to influence the heart and mind, so our responsibility is to read and study. It is the Holy Spirit that makes the changes.

My mom used to say, "God holds you accountable for the amount of light He has given you. Live according to what He has shown you." We can't wait to know it all before we begin to obey. My journey of obedience is different than yours. We mustn't judge anyone else. What do you know at this time in your life? Obey what you know. Share what He teaches. God will reveal more to you when you need more understanding and wisdom.

The phrase, "Don't rush the fruit," is a reminder for parents (of biological children or spiritual ones,) to patiently teach and train, with spiritual maturity as the ultimate goal in mind. Spend time in God's Word. Remember, we can't change ourselves nor our children. We can trust God to change all our lives. That is GRACE.

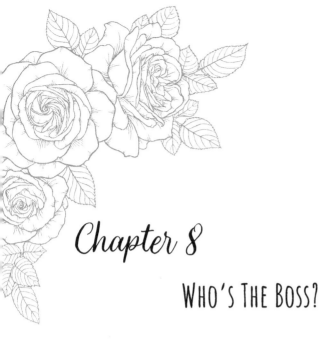

Chapter 8

WHO'S THE BOSS?

Allow me to share an analogy that has helped me better understand my role as a parent in the lives of my children. This all started when one of my daughters went for a weekend to the home of a college friend. This friend, Mary, had a horse by the name of Flicka. As Liz sat watching Mary work with her horse, she was fascinated by the interaction between horse and owner.

Mary brought Flicka out of the barn into the corral. She attached a lead rope, and while facing the horse and moving backwards, she spoke quietly as they walked. After a few trips around the corral, she turned her back to Flicka and continued to speak as she led her around the fenced-in area.

After a few more trips around the corral, Mary faced her horse again. This time she removed the lead rope and while continuing to speak to her, led Flicka with just her voice. Finally, Mary turned her back to the horse and just stood, quietly waiting. When the horse finally came and put its head on her shoulder, she knew the horse would follow her anywhere.

As I was listening to Liz describe her experience, I had this thought, "*This is a lot like parenting.*" We lead our children with our words, exerting a certain amount of authority, like the lead rope used with Flicka. My husband used to tell our younger children, "Listen to me with your eyes!" We needed to know they were really listening and ready to obey. As they grow up, our children will need our teaching to give them direction, and they still need some overt authority to help them learn to obey. There is a growing relationship that earns parents the right to lead.

As children reach later elementary ages and early adolescence, they still need teaching, but there is a greater focus on helping them learn to submit their own wills to the expanding authorities in their lives. They are beginning to make some of their own decisions. We can give counsel and training, but obedience comes from the strength of the parent-child relationship. This is like Mary removing the lead rope and continuing to direct the horse. She faced her while continuing to speak, and led her in the safety of the corral.

Finally, as our children approach adulthood, our role in training becomes that of a counselor; the need for parental authority is diminishing. The young adult begins to act based on past training and experience. Mary waited for Flicka to come behind her, willing to follow her without coercion. Their interaction was based on the relationship that had developed.

I felt excited as I saw this as a great analogy and pattern for working with my kids. The process of teaching obedience takes time and patience. I had always thought God allowed us as parents to teach our kids to obey us, as practice for eventually obeying Him.

But then, almost like a slap on the face, God stopped me.

"You've got this all wrong. I am the owner! You are just the lead rope."

Oh! I had gotten it all wrong. God uses us as parents, as a tool, like the lead rope, to teach them to follow HIM. I am not asked to train them to follow me! His commands and instructions are the words I should speak, so they learn to trust and submit to His Will. God's goal is for my children to hear His voice on their own and to follow Him in love, with all their heart, soul, mind, and strength. Their yielding to His plans is based on their relationship to Him.

It is hard to give up what we have always felt was our singular responsibility to manage these children we love. We are still accountable to God for what we teach. We must learn to trust Him to lead them into adulthood. He knows everything, including how to best reach their hearts and direct their lives. How much better for them to follow the One who will never leave them nor forsake them. Their relationship with Him will be eternal.

Respect for authority is an essential attitude to teach. The ultimate authority is God Himself. "I am the Lord, your God. You shall have no other gods before Me," says the first commandment.

We need to yield the right to make all our own plans and to choose our own priorities. This is a lifelong fight against the desire to be our own boss.

This starts when a child is very young. He tests out his new language, "No" or "Do it myself!" Then the battle for getting what a child wants intensifies. "I want that car," when another toy is put before him. We can acknowledge preferences, and allow kids some practice in making decisions, but we shouldn't set ourselves up for a repeated power struggle.

This could seem like a minor matter and it is often easier to just give in as a parent or grandparent, rather than fight a battle. This takes discernment. The underlying issue is a child's attitude of being willing to yield. Some children are more compliant than others. For some children, outward submission can hide an inner rebellion. Look at patterns in a child's response when their request is denied. Be patient, yet resolved in encouraging a better response. God wants us to lead more like shepherds with their sheep, than like ranchers driving their cattle.

When we needed to leave some of our younger kids with a babysitter or maybe an older sibling, we learned we had to make clear for all the kids just who was in charge. We would ask the kids, "Who is the number one boss?" They all knew the answer. "God!" "Who is the number two boss?" "Daddy." "Who is the number three boss?" "Mommy." "Who is the number four boss?" The answer was whoever Dad and Mom left in charge. We explained that the number four boss is left by Mom and Dad to help keep them safe. If they didn't follow our instructions to the babysitter, we would treat it like they were disobeying us.

God wants us to respect those in authority over us. We are to pray for those in authority. Sometimes we have to be reminded that whether or not we know or even like a person, their position requires respect. Obviously, parents and authority figures are not perfect. We are all damaged by sin. Tragically, there are too many examples of people who misuse their power to take advantage of someone under their influence. We need our children to know that God's authority comes first. If someone asks for actions contrary to God's moral law, they need to refuse. Remember when the apostles were commanded "to speak no more of Jesus," in Acts 5:28. Peter replied, "We must obey God rather than men."

So how can we help our children be respectful when they disagree with someone in charge, including parents? When it is a matter of ethics and obedience to God, there is no choice but to take a stand. We can teach them a respectful way to respond. This is not our original idea. It comes from the example of Daniel in Babylon.

Daniel and some of his fellow Jewish youths had been taken captive in Israel. They were taken to Babylon to become servants in King Nebuchadnezzar's court. They were to be trained in language, literature, knowledge, and understanding, in order to prepare them for personal service to the king. They were to be given everything they needed for a three-year training program, including the same rich food as the king. "Daniel made up his mind that he would not defile himself with the king's food or drink." (Daniel 1:8) He had rules for his diet that were set by God and he wanted to stay obedient, even in this foreign country.

Daniel sought permission from the commander of the officials to follow a different diet, so that he could live by Jewish laws. The official did not want to fail his king by not producing healthy, successful young men. His own life was at stake. Daniel made a suggestion.

> "Please test your servants for ten days and let us be given some vegetables to eat and water to drink. Then let our appearance be observed in your presence and the appearance of the youths who are eating the king's choice food; Deal with your servants according to what you see." (Daniel 1:12-13)

Daniel made a reasonable request. He understood the end goal but suggested another option for himself and his friends.

What was the result? At the end of the ten days, their appearance seemed better than the others. The official allowed them to continue with their own diet. At the end of the time of preparation, the king interviewed these Jewish youths. Out of them all, "not one was found like Daniel and his three friends. As for every matter of wisdom and understanding, he found them ten times better than all the magicians and conjurers (advisors), he had all across his realm." (Daniel 1:20) God had given them what they needed and blessed their obedience.

How does that apply today? When any of our children disagreed about a decision we had made as parents, they were allowed to ask us to reconsider our decision once. They could give us the information they thought we had missed or not considered. They could make the case for a change. The agreement was that we would pray about it again with their new input. They in turn would trust us to decide as God gave us peace. They would have to agree to accept our decision respectfully. Growing Kids, God's Way called this "a respectful appeal."

My favorite story about this arrangement concerns one of our daughters. She was in her junior year of high school. She told us she wanted a greater challenge in school. She was home-schooled but also took a class at the local high school which allowed her to participate on the track team. She really wanted us to put her in the public school for her last year and a half. We prayed about it but didn't sense that this was the right direction to go. She strongly felt we were not considering all her concerns. Her letter of appeal was a legal brief. We prayed about it some more but still felt her first choice was not the best decision for her.

We gave her three choices to consider. Mary could take online college classes for her next semester, knowing that she would then have enough high school credits to graduate that spring. Choice number two was to apply to the public school to allow her to attend the second semester as a senior. We would ask that she be allowed to graduate in the spring. The third choice was to attend a Christian boarding school out of state, also as a senior who would graduate in the spring. We knew she was really ready to go to college, so this gave her three options to lead to the challenge she needed.

Our daughter chose to try the local high school first. I appealed to the school, asking them to let her take a full load of classes and graduate. They said they had so many more classes she could take, so they would not allow her to graduate that year. With that closed door, our daughter wanted us to contact the out of state school. She had friends already there. Mary had been accepted that past summer to attend in the fall, but we didn't have the money to send her. I called the school to ask if they would allow her to come mid-year and still graduate in the spring. Three of our other children had already gone there for their senior year and graduated, so the school board decided to let her come.

We had about three weeks to make all our arrangements. After setting her up in the dorm, I went to the finance office to figure out how to begin paying her bill. The secretary told me that someone had already paid it for us. My heart was over-whelmed by God's provision through an anonymous donor. I went to tell my daughter. She answered, "This was obviously the Lord's leading. I need to make the most of my time here."

Learning to approach authorities with respect is very important for our children, especially in the teen years. Obviously, this option can also be adjusted to address disagree-ments with a boss or teacher, even between us as adults. The key is respect and a willingness to trust God to work in our lives, even if we don't get the outcome for which we hope.

We often focus on the respect from a child to a parent, but there is also a need to show respect for the thinking of our maturing children. I learned from experience that I often made wrong assumptions about a child's response of "WHY?" My reaction to that question caused frustration for one of my kids. I assumed he was challenging my authority when I gave some instructions. There seemed to be constant friction when I accused him of challenging me. He finally explained that most of the time he was really asking for an explanation. He just wanted more information. He was right. He needed to understand better what I was expecting and why. When I gave a rational reason for an instruction, it made it easier for him to comply. I had to learn to explain and he had to be careful how he asked for more information, because the tone of voice can communicate disrespect. I think this is especially true for our boys as they begin to think and reason as young men. My son needed to be respected for his perspectives and ideas. I needed to recognize he was now accountable to God directly for his choices. I needed to step out of the way as I was being removed, like the lead rope in our story.

I have come to believe that past generations had a better grasp of the maturing process for our kids. We seem to think keeping them children as long as we can is a gift we can give them. We hold off giving them responsibilities and try to protect them from any pain or disappointment. This can be crippling as our children move to adulthood. By the time our kids are twelve or thirteen, and for some even earlier, they need to be told they are accountable to God for their choices. They need to answer to God for their actions just like adults. They still have to earn adult privileges by their behavior. We need to evaluate the evidence of each individual's maturity.

What does it mean to be mature? Remember God's description from Hebrews 5:14. Someone is mature when "because of practice, they have their senses trained to discern good and evil." This is the time to encourage our children to read and study the Bible. Take time for discussions about God's standards of good and evil and what that looks like in our generation. The Holy Spirit will be the one to help them discern the difference and to learn to examine their own choices using His unchanging standards. If you remember the Horse Lesson, this is where God is using His own voice to lead our children, and we as the lead rope are being needed less and less. Isn't that the ultimate goal, to see our children following God from their hearts?

"I have no greater joy than this, to hear of my children walking in the truth." (3 John 1:4)

Chapter 9
A Great Work Ethic Doesn't Just Happen

If there is one thing for which my children have expressed appreciation, it is that they learned how to work early in life. My own parents required us to do weekly chores, usually on Saturday morning. We were taught that this was part of participating in a family. We were not given an allowance for the chores we did. Everyone was expected to share in the work it takes to live together.

We were five children in a row house in Brooklyn, sharing two bedrooms. There were seven of us sharing one bathroom. We were taught how to clean up after ourselves and to leave a place cleaner than we found it. That standard was expected to carry into our personal space, our family dwelling, and even into public facilities. It was considered courtesy to not leave a mess for others to clean up.

When the doorbell rang announcing an unexpected visitor, anyone who was home was expected to drop what he was doing and run to the living room. Each child was expected to pick up at least two things and put them away. That meant ten items moved in one minute to make the living room ready to receive guests. We were told this was part of being hospitable; that is, to not expect a guest to move our books, toys or games so they could visit our mom or dad. We had no playroom or family room where those things could have been used, so our living space was basically a living room connected to a dining room and a shared bedroom. It is no surprise that playing outside was always encouraged.

When we were old enough to take small jobs, we watched neighbors' pets, did some housekeeping tasks, babysat, washed cars, etc. My parents encouraged us to be willing to work. I remember wanting to give the oldest of my kids the chance to earn some of their own money. Maybe that money could be used for those Christmas presents they wanted to buy for each other. Sometimes they were saving for something that was more than our budget could afford, like a bike or toy or later on, better basketball shoes. I made a series of index cards with jobs that could be done by a child, with the price I was willing to pay for their work. My son, Jon, who was already an entrepreneur at six years of age, looked at my jobs and pay scale and frankly said I wasn't paying enough for the work. He probably was right but that's what I could afford.

They soon were old enough to do paper routes, which not only paid more but also taught the reality that you have to fulfill your commitments. Rain, snow, below freezing temperatures, and even lack of sleep were not an excuse to skip delivery. We were living in the upper Midwest at the time and winters were brutal. Papers came to the house every morning by five and had to be delivered by eight at the latest, seven days a week, 365 days a year.

One day, while watching a baseball game on TV, the announcer was talking about the rules that governed when the bat boys and girls could work. There were child labor laws for their jobs. My kids started questioning why there were no labor laws for paper carriers. They worked early morning hours and in all weather conditions. We would often have to follow them on their routes on some winter mornings when the real temperature was -30 degrees. They could only do two houses before they would come back in the car to warm up. They sometimes had to deliver in a blizzard, even when the post offices were closed. After one crazy blizzard, our mailman came to the door with a pile of mail that had collected over a few days. He thanked our kids for getting him his newspaper every day, while he was stuck at home.

The only time anyone missed delivering the paper was when a flu hit our family. Thankfully, it was spring! Three of the kids had routes, and one of those had a second. All were really sick, including my husband. As you can probably guess, I had to make all the deliveries for two days. One of those routes was new for my son. It was really dark in the morning and I couldn't see the house numbers. Jon had to sit in the front seat of our car, sick as could be, and point out the houses and apartments that were his customers and explain where they wanted their paper placed. Yes, this was delivery right to the door or inside the door or in a box, etc. I drove the first day and walked most of the second. I remember someone asking why the paper was late … I just shook my head … I was too tired to answer.

As the kids got older, they each rejoiced when they could give up their paper routes for "a real job." They had learned about responsibility and even the consequences of doing a job poorly. They also learned about finishing well, even when someone takes advantage of you. My younger son was asked to do some yard work and grunt work in the house of someone in the neighborhood. He said yes to the yard work at one wage. When the homeowner saw how hard he worked, he asked him to do more projects. David did things like bleaching the walls of a shed covered in mildew, pulling up carpets, and repairing some stairs, etc. My son thought he should have been paid more for some of those jobs. Then he found out that the man had scheduled a local home repair person to do those jobs but would have had to pay a lot more to use the service. He canceled the company and had David do it for a lot less. That was a lesson in not being bitter but finishing what you agreed to do, and finishing well.

The youngest two girls of our family did not have to do paper routes. We had moved to the East by then. They did some church cleaning to earn some extra money. Another daughter became a lifeguard. She worked at YMCA pools and taught private lessons. Eventually, she became a certified trainer for lifeguards in New Jersey. When the opportunity came to earn school money by working at the college pool, she took the job. It led to more work at a local YMCA. She took off a year of college to earn money for school and was hired to manage the Aquatics Program for that YMCA. She had to hire, train, do scheduling, managing payroll, and setting budgets. Those skills became what she needed for work in her final years of college. She was hired to do a job in the finance office of her school. Her experience in the nonprofit world, and then in other businesses, equipped her for a financial consulting job, right out of college.

Eventually, for the youngest girls, there was work at a nearby Conference Center when we moved to Pennsylvania. They did housekeeping, and served as wait staff in the dining room. Eventually they had jobs in several other food service establishments. God used those jobs to provide summer income they would need to help pay for college. Each child has their own story of God's provision for finances and for skills that have become part of their lives now as adults.

Children and youth also need to learn how to relate to customers and clients. The customer is not always right, but they need to be treated respectfully anyway. Going the extra mile makes an impression. We had a funny lesson with two of our kids that taught this principle. Mary and David were doing paper routes in North Dakota. This was an afternoon paper delivery. Mary was in fifth grade and walked her way through her route. Sometimes, she stopped to talk to one of her elderly customers and still finished on time. David had other commitments. He had to get his route done after finishing his school work for the day, in time to get to football or basketball practice at the local public school. He would go as fast as he could, often riding his bike to cover the distance quickly. One day, close to Christmas, David came home from his route and showed us his plastic bag of returned rubber bands, left as tips for Christmas. There were other tips but these made him laugh. That was until Mary came home with her cash and gifts. There were no rubber bands. The lesson? Relationships matter in business. Take the time.

Whether a task is part of a job or part of school or ministry, we need to teach and train our kids when they are young, to work hard and finish well. Too many times, we are tempted to show compassion and maybe excuse a child when she just doesn't feel like doing something. How often when the demands increase do we hear, "I just want to quit!" I have seen it in sports, in summer jobs, in music lessons, or even relationships. As parents and teachers, we need to help them persevere. Liz has often said that her dad's words to her have stayed with her even till today. She wanted to quit swimming lessons, and he wouldn't let her. "We have to finish what we start." Of course, if there really is a specific health concern, or a serious reason to pull out, they have to exit properly. Otherwise, kids need to finish the season. semester or commitment. They need to think before making a commitment—Do *NOT* promise what you are *NOT* willing to finish.

As much as we can instill a sense of satisfaction in our kids to be contributors to the resources of the family and to experience the dignity of doing a good day's work, to that end, our children will look for responsible ways to provide for themselves. They will hopefully have some extra money to help a ministry, or someone in need. God means for us to have compassion, but He also wants those who can work, to work for their daily needs. The widow and orphan in Israel were allowed to pick up extra grain along the harvested fields without having to pay but they had to at least get up and gather.

There is dignity in work. God meant it to be so. He gave Adam and Eve work to do in the perfect Garden of Eden, *before* there was sin in the world. It was meant to be honorable. We need to restore that attitude so our own children and grandchildren learn to be responsible and prepared with the skills and resources to do what God will ask of them.

Chapter 10

STATION WAGON STRATEGIES

One of the top priorities for us as a family was spending quality time with extended family members. This was important to my family, since my father had only a few of his family here in the United States. My mom's family all lived fairly close to each other, except for one enterprising brother who moved to California from the New York area. As long as my grandfather was alive, we would meet somewhere in Pennsylvania for a yearly reunion. As we grandchildren grew and married, the reunions continued but rarely could everyone get there every year. Most of our family trips as mom and dad and seven children were planned around when that family gathering was scheduled to happen.

Since our family moved almost every four or five years as God changed the congregation we were serving, those summer trips were the means to keep our kids in touch with their cousins. This meant driving all nine of us from the Midwest to either the New York–New Jersey area or Seattle, Washington. We could never afford plane tickets or other transportation, nor could we really afford a hotel along the way. So our nine-passenger station wagon was both hotel and amusement center on our approximately fifteen-hundred-mile drives.

This yearly adventure took some advanced planning on my part, if the travel time was also going to be a happy part of the vacation. I began gathering targeted surprises to hand out when needed. They would provide a needed distraction or a constructive activity for a daily quiet hour after lunch. When the kids were young, I would have the tools for a puppet show in my bag. At first that just meant a few sock puppets with button eyes and yarn hair. Eventually, I found a few premade puppets, a kitten and a puppy, that were my fictional characters. As the kids grew up, some of the older kids took over the storytelling to engage their siblings for periods of time. To be honest, several of the kids should have recorded and published their stories. No one wanted to miss a single moment or detail of the stories being told.

We also found recorded stories for everyone to enjoy. The Adventures in Odyssey series was always a favorite. They provided hours of suspense and laughter. I found other audio books that were biographies or fictional series that allowed the kids to use their imagination as they listened. Sometimes, I read books aloud, chapter by chapter, stretching the story over the many miles and hours. As the kids grew up, they loved to read for themselves. I would order a few new stories or sequels to something they were already reading. When teasing went too far or someone got fidgety, I would open my bag in the front seat and hand out a new book or activity. A pad of sticky notes and a pencil provided hours of drawing and then decorating the seat or window nearby. Coloring books and crayons, Word Search, Sudoku, or a book of mazes were ready to change the focus to something positive.

Of course, there were food and snack surprises. I learned to only have small water bottles to pass out in order to minimize the bathroom stops. It also kept the sticky spills to a minimum. We usually had our first meal of sandwiches and fruit ready in a cooler. We could make good progress in the first four to five hours. My favorite fruit was grapes; I called them God's little juice boxes. I packaged them in individual Ziploc bags so I could hand them out as needed.

We learned that leaving on a trip right after supper meant everyone was satisfied and somewhat tired from their day. The kids seemed to settle down for the long trip as soon as we packed into the car. We would leave while it was still daylight, giving the kids time to look out the window, play license plate games, or just enjoy the scenery. By the time we took our first gas/bathroom break, we were hours on the way. I had the kids change into pajamas and eat our quick supper, and the daylight was gone. Everyone made themselves as comfortable as possible in their assigned seats and by the time they woke up, it was 8:00 am and time for breakfast.

We had accomplished more than a third of our drive time, and the kids were refreshed, fed, changed into clean clothes, and given something to do for the beginning of the day. At the first sign of discontent, we could use a story or some other group game. The kids could nap on and off that day. Usually by suppertime, everyone knew we were almost there. We started looking out for the familiar scenery, or road signs and land-marks. The car trip itself had become part of the fun. Even as the kids got older, they would ask, "When are we going to take another trip when we can sleep in the car?"

Here are two additional tips for traveling with kids. First, we had limited luggage space, so everyone had one small duffel bag in which to pack their clothes. Those were put in the back till we reached our destination. They each had a small backpack they filled with whatever they chose to use on the trip, i.e. cars, a stuffed animal, a book, etc. They also had their pj's and a morning change of clothes to save us time finding what they needed for our twenty-four-hour travel day. Everyone had a pillow and a blanket to make themselves comfortable as they slept.

Second, everyone had assigned seats, which changed depending on how kids were relating at different stages of life. Usually, there was a car seat in the middle of the center and back bench seats, which became a natural marker for personal space. I could place an older child next to each toddler or infant to help with childcare. They could handle the bottles, entertainment, and, sometimes singing to soothe a restless little one. That helped me, since I was going to have to drive the night shift and needed to catch some sleep before I took over. We all knew that David, the middle child, was going to sit in the front seat between Dan and myself. His job was to pass snacks to his dad to keep him awake so I could actually sleep. David would be his dad's conversation partner. He often says his job was to keep the whole family alive! What a responsibility! We couldn't have done it without you, Dave!

To this day, my kids seem to have an automatic travel switch that gets triggered on long trips. Even their spouses know they can sleep anywhere, anytime, whenever the car pulls out of the driveway. They have also learned to drive long distances, especially to get to a time with family and friends. I am thankful they are giving family time a high priority.

A year ago, Rachel arranged for a Zoom event, "Cousins Got Talent." This allowed the kids to share something from their hard work in school, or piano recital pieces, and voice lesson songs with each other, especially since no one could participate in live recitals. Even the little ones could sing a song or tell a joke. The kids from Cambodia could participate with their cousins in Minnesota, California, and New Jersey. Even great grandparents in Washington could join the event and get to know these children a little better.

These grandkids can know their cousins who are now spread across the globe. It takes effort and even budgeted finances to make it happen whenever possible. I love watching them gather together, playing games, doing puzzles, cooking in the kitchen, doing dishes, etc. They are building memories and choosing to love each other.

Chapter 11

OUR MEMORIAL SHELF—TELL ME THE STORY!

"One generation shall praise Your works to another and
shall declare Your mighty acts."
(Psalm 145:4)

What does God want our children and grandchildren to know? This answer provides our greatest treasure to leave for our families and friends. Start with telling what God has done for you!

One practical tool someone suggested to use to tell your family's story is a memorial book. The idea comes from the Old Testament. The Lord told Joshua to write down in a book of memorials what God had done for Israel. This was so the following generations would know what God had already done and would learn to trust Him. They set up stone monuments to prompt the retelling of many national events.

Some people have used a photo book to record their stories. We have a shelf in our entryway with items that prompt the telling of our family stories. "Why do you have that item on the shelf?" kids have asked. My answer? "Oh, I am so glad you asked. Let me tell you something God did for us." Then I get to tell about specific answers to prayer or special opportunities He gave to a member of our family. Usually, when I've finished one story, they ask about everything on the shelf. How fun to give God the credit He deserves! Here are some examples.

We lived on a limited budget, partly by choice. I chose to invest in educating my children and to help at the churches my husband served as pastor. That meant we often had to ask some hard questions about what we could afford. These questions are important so I will repeat. "Is this a need or is this a want?" The answer was usually to pray about it first and ask God to provide what He wanted us to have. We had a dry-erase board in the kitchen, behind the door, where only our family could see it. When an item was on the list, we would pray and wait. Sometimes, the item was taken off the list and we accepted that God's answer was "No." Learning to take a "No" was important for all of us to accept. Maybe God had another plan. Sometimes, the answer was "Yes" and the answer was often provided in a miraculous way so we couldn't miss His hand in it. Let me tell you about Becky's shoes.

During one specific season in our family's journey when we had four children, we had just moved from the East Coast to the Midwest. We had to spend what we did have just to fill the empty refrigerator and cupboards. My oldest daughter, about ten years old, had outgrown her tennis shoes and really needed new ones. We prayed about it, and Becky went to write it on the kitchen prayer board. As she left the kitchen to come back for school, the doorbell rang. She answered the door and a stranger stood there with a pair of purple tennis shoes.

The woman asked, "Could anyone in your family use these shoes?"

Becky said, "Thank you. I will try them on." Of course, they fit her perfectly.

The woman said, "Great. They're yours," and she left.

We never saw her again. You can be sure my children learned a powerful lesson about God's ability to provide for our needs. I eventually found a pair of Barbie sneakers that were almost purple and put them on our Memorial Shelf, so we wouldn't forget to be thankful.

My husband has his own fun stories of God's provision. He had been asked to spend a week at a Christian camp in New Hampshire as the Bible teacher for a group of college students. Dan had mostly dress clothes since he wore a shirt and tie most of his time in ministry. This camp was going to require more casual clothing, which he did not have. Dan and I sat down at a table one Saturday evening and wrote a list of the barest essentials he would need to do this ministry. Only he and I knew about this list. Then we prayed for God's provision, since we couldn't afford this extra expense.

That next morning, in the offering plate, was an envelope with Dan's name written on it. Inside was a gift certificate to a local men's clothing store. With amazement, we took the list we had made and went to the store where this was issued. We were able to purchase everything on the list with less than a dollar to spare. We praised God with renewed faith in His concern for us as a family. We couldn't thank the donor, because it was anonymously given. We have some "toy" men's clothing on our Memorial Shelf to remind us of that time in our life. May God continue to build faith in all of us, and may He receive the glory!

Another item on our Memorial Shelf is a white toy station wagon. Years ago, our family was on a trip to pick up two of our kids from a summer Bible camp. We were going to join them there for a family weekend that followed their camp. We were excited to spend that time with some people from our former church along with their families. The drive would take about six hours.

As we finished four hours of that trip, the weather changed and there was a torrential downpour. Our station wagon started to have a problem. My husband needed to pull off on the closest exit. As we sat in the storm with the car full of luggage and five other children, we were stuck. We prayed for God to help us in this dilemma, knowing that our kids at camp would be wondering where we were. This was before cell phones were available to everyone.

While we were still praying, someone knocked on the driver's window. We were startled! Dan opened the window. Standing there in the pouring rain was a uniformed man asking if we needed help. It turned out he was the chief of police from a city not too far away. He said, "I don't know why I pulled off at this exit. I usually get off on the next one." After assessing the situation, he called a tow truck from a local repair shop and went with us to that garage. He also called his wife and asked her to meet us there with their minivan. By the time she arrived, we had emptied the car, and Dan had arranged for our car to be repaired while we were at camp.

The police officer helped us load up his van with all our stuff and children. He drove us to the house of our family friends, about an hour away, where we could borrow a car for the rest of the trip. We were so thankful for the good Samaritan who stopped to help us on that stormy day.

God was not done with providing for us that weekend. We had called from our friend's house to tell the kids why we were late and to expect us later that evening. Our friends who were already at the camp asked where we were, so the kids explained our absence. By the time we got there, it was time for bed.

The next morning, one of the couples we were to meet pulled us aside. They told us that when we were part of their congregation, God had put on their hearts to buy us a car. They just didn't find the right time to arrange it. They felt God was asking them to do it now. They instructed us to find a vehicle that would meet the needs of our family and told us the amount they were offering.

Before we headed home, we found out that the car we left for repairs could not be fixed for the long term. We were able to drive it home but absolutely needed another vehicle. God provided a white nine-passenger station wagon at the price our friends had offered. God had led another family to be good Samaritans in our time of distress. We are so thankful to them and to God.

I found a small matchbox station wagon which I painted white, to put on our shelf and to remind us that God knows what we need, even before we do. I could tell the stories of several cars God provided in fun ways, when we really needed one. I don't have space to tell all those stories. If you are one of those who did so, please know we have thanked God many times for your gift. Those stories bring a strengthening of faith to our family and to those who have heard of your kindness. Thank you again!

Sometimes we have the chance to leave a legacy of encouragement to people beyond our own families. What a blessing to cheer someone or remind them that others care and are concerned! How many groups have made hats for newborns in the hospital? Some have made lap blankets for the elderly in a nursing home. How many of us have filled shoe boxes with something to bless a child on the other side of the world? The hope is that they would understand God's gift of Jesus and His great love for them through the love of His people.

The Jews were told to build altars or to hold yearly festivals to remember God's commands or displays of power. The feast of the Passover was one such festival. Every year, families would repeat the story of God's deliverance from Egypt and slavery. They were to remember God's power and His promise to continue to provide for them.

Here is another way women would often pass on family memories. They would make quilts with fabric from no longer usable clothing. Grandma might sit and tell her grandchildren about the woman who wore a dress for a special occasion and point to the square that came from that garment. The simple history of a family would be passed on with something tangible. A quilt often became a treasured heirloom shared across generations. We received such a treasured quilt from a congregation in North Dakota.

Our family moved every three to five years, as my husband, Dan, accepted calls to minister to several congregations. At one time, now as a family with seven children, we were packing to leave again from a beloved congregation. Several of our kids were now teenagers. Someone arranged with ladies of the church to make a quilt for our farewell. It had been signed by many of the congregation. Words of blessing, prayers, love, and affirmation filled the squares. When we arrived at our new home, I put that quilt on the bed in one of the rooms. I watched as the kids congregated on that bed, during many days and evenings. They read aloud the greetings and names of these gracious people. That quilt soothed the sadness of those early days, as we had to start over again to get to know people in our new church and to begin to make new friends. I am so thankful for that quilt of comfort and the reminder of God's love through His people.

God works in each of our lives on different issues and in different ways. Each of us will have a collection of stories to tell. We get to leave the stories of how God personally acts on our behalf as a treasure for the next generation. Be ready to pass on the stories of what He has done for you.

Chapter 12

Good, Better, Best

"What does it profit a man to gain the whole world and forfeit his soul?" (Mark 8:36)

𝓔very day, we are faced with choices. Do we invest in a new business venture, maybe from home? Do we commit time and effort to further our education? Maybe we want to slim down to look like we did ten years ago. None of the previous options is foolish or without some benefit. But any of these pursuits could replace some greater priorities that need our time and treasure.

Was this not what Jesus was modeling on a visit to Martha and Mary's home? Martha needed help for the preparation and serving of food for their guests, but Mary sat at Jesus' feet listening to His teaching. He said to Martha, "only one thing is necessary, for Mary has chosen the good part, which shall not be taken away from her." (Luke 10:42) Jesus' time on earth was short, and learning from Him was the most important thing she could do. How many of us would love to sit physically at His feet today? With all the demands for our attention, we need to be intentional about choosing the best things.

I remember when I had only one little one at home to nurture. I wanted so much to be a good mother. I turned on what at the time was the premiere radio broadcast on parenting, "Focus on The Family." I had so much to learn. Unfortunately, I found myself getting impatient with my little girl when I couldn't hear the broadcast over her innocent playing and noise. When it dawned on me what was happening, I felt ashamed. I realized I had to make a choice – nurture my daughter or educate myself. I committed to keep the radio off when she was awake. I learned later on to ask myself, "Is this the time? Is this the place?" I found other resources and chose another time to learn.

There are other situations when we may need to postpone something important. My husband and I learned that if we had a difference of opinion about an issue or a need to discipline a child, Saturday night was a terrible time to deal with it. We agreed to postpone emotional issues until after Sunday morning ministries. The issue could be very important, but waiting did not mean we didn't take it seriously. Of course, life and death issues can't wait, nor matters of imminent danger. We would ask, "Is this the time? Is this the place?" Most of our postponed discussions had a better and more rational resolution.

When I was almost sixty years old, someone offered me the chance to take a course related to Christian Education. I struggled with feeling "old" and began to wonder if I still had a reason to invest in another training opportunity. I started to wonder if I still had something of value to contribute. I was reminded of a verse I had used with my fourth and fifth grade classes. The lesson was to warn them about wasting their upcoming teen years instead of using them wisely.

"So teach us to number our days, that we may present to You a heart of wisdom." (Psalm 90:12) I tried to number the possible days left to me, should the Lord allow me to live to the same age as my parents. I would have maybe twenty years left. That is approximately 7,300 days. I didn't want to waste any of them!

I asked God to guide my heart as I tried to make decisions about continuing in ministry. I happened to pick up a devotional called "Our Daily Bread." The title of the meditation for that day was "Too Old?" You can be sure I read it. It was talking about Caleb who was one of the spies Moses sent into Canaan to survey the land God was giving Israel. After the forty years of wandering in the wilderness, Caleb was eighty years old. He said he was just as strong as he was at forty and would drive out the Anakim in the land. These were giants that the younger men had failed to defeat. The quote on the bottom of the page said, "When God adds years to your life, ask Him to add life to your years." In other words, live to the full doing what He leads you to do. Age has nothing to do with fruitfulness!

I had been doing children's ministries for many years. I was getting tired and wondered if it was time to step aside. Age was not to be the deciding factor. The Lord moved my heart to see how important these children, these young ones, are to Him. It was as if He said to not look down on the small part I could play. If I could turn the hearts of these little ones to know Him and love Him, it could give them a whole lifetime to serve Him. That was an investment worth making. I needed that fresh sense of purpose.

If there is one treasure I could pass on to the children in our church, it is a love for God's Word. "This book of the law shall not depart from your mouth, but you shall meditate on it day and night, so that you may be careful to do according to all that is written in it; for then you will make your way prosperous, and then you will have success." (Joshua 1:8)

I always loved to read. I sometimes used a flashlight under my blanket at night to "just finish a chapter." The older I got, the more I realized the influence books could have on me. I read an autobiography of Hudson Taylor who had gone to China to be a missionary. The book was filled with his diaries and letters. I remember his words to his sister in England warning her of being too attached to books. He quoted Solomon in Ecclesiastes 12:12, "... be warned; the writing of many books is endless and excessive devotion to books is wearying to the body."

Good literature has value. There is much to learn and understand. But if we want to choose what is going to be the best material to feed our souls, it must be the Bible. Someone used the analogy that a good book is like a quick snack on the run. It satisfies a momentary craving. God's Word is like a banquet of choice foods prepared and served by God Himself. It nourishes and provides what is healthy and satisfying.

My dad loved to share a verse from the Bible when he was particularly moved by its message. He would often wake us up early in the morning before he left for work, to say good-bye. Sometimes he shared some expression of praise that had filled his heart. Mom had her time with the Lord after all the kids left for school. She would sit at the small kitchen table with her coffee and her Bible. Several times a week, her sister who lived downstairs would join her and they would share a special time with each other and the Lord.

I know God used their faith to put a fresh hunger in my heart to understand His Word. I began to ask, "If God really means what He says (and He does!), then how should that affect how I live?" The words of God became tools to convict me of sin and to turn my heart to repent. The Bible is where I find wisdom for life. I want my children to read it and study it for themselves!

I made sure each child had a Bible of his own when he was able to read. Sometimes, the church provided one for each Sunday School child. Often, I picked a version they could understand and that had a larger type that would be easy on their eyes. I encouraged them to read from Genesis to Revelations and tried to follow their progress. If there was a section that I knew needed to be skipped at a certain age, I stepped in and edited as I read it for them. Sometimes, when they came down during my own quiet time, I would share with them what I was learning. I showed those who were interested how to use some tools in my study Bible, to look up the Greek or Hebrew definitions to clarify a section that was difficult to understand. I can't remember how many times I had to go to Sarah's room to find my Bible since she had taken it to use for her own devotions. Eventually, we bought one for her like mine.

"So will My Word be which goes forth from My mouth; It will not return to Me empty, without accomplishing what I desire, and without succeeding in the matter for which I sent it!" (Isaiah 55:11)

What a promise! God's Word always accomplishes His purposes. If we are going to share some word of truth, we should use what we know has eternal value. We will never fully understand all that can be found in God's Word, at least during our earthly life, but God wants us to seek to know and obey each piece of truth He has given. God delights in our search for wisdom.

This makes me think of my dad. He would toss coins ahead of us when we were out for a walk. He would tell us to keep our eyes open to find the treasures others may have lost. He modeled this for us. He would often find watches, rings, money, and even someone's car that had been stolen. We would love to run up to him with our treasure and he was quick to celebrate with us when we found something. To this day, I watch the sidewalk or street expecting to see a penny or a dime and I remember those times with him. I think God is a lot like that. He has scattered treasures for us to discover. The more intently we look, the more we will find. He, too, as our great Father, rejoices with our discoveries.

Chapter 13

To Speak Or Not To Speak

"To be or not to be." was Shakespeare's question spoken by Hamlet. The character in this tragedy was struggling with having the will to live in the midst of great turmoil. He so longed for peace, yet he feared the unknown of what an escape into eternity through death might bring. He was afraid of death.

I often ask a similar question, "To speak or not to speak?" Communication can be such a difficult part of our relationships. I think Solomon has given us many wise principles to help us navigate the maze of words. He makes a similar point when he says there is, "a time to be silent and a time to speak." (Ecclesiastes 3:7) Crying out to the Lord for wisdom is always appropriate. Before we speak and offer wisdom to others, we need to get help from the Lord Himself. His Spirit prompts us to speak but can also warn us to be silent. As children, we were told that God gave us two ears and one mouth. The suggestion was made that we should listen twice as much as we speak. This seems like a good balance.

"If you cry for discernment, lift your voice for understanding; if you seek her as silver and search for her as for hidden treasures; Then you will discern the fear of the Lord and discover the knowledge of God. For the Lord gives wisdom ..."
(Proverbs 2:3–5)

"This you know, my beloved brethren. but everyone must be quick to hear, slow to speak, and slow to anger, for the anger of man does not achieve the righteousness of God."
(James 1:19–20)

Sometimes, I became overwhelmed with all the demands of homeschooling and ministry. I felt like a failure every time I gave in to an angry response to something with the kids. It certainly wasn't very effective in solving a problem. I would sometimes have seasons of fatigue that seemed to lead to seasons of impatience. I remember reading the previous verse from James 1. The last phrase got my undivided attention. "The anger of man (or mother) does not achieve the righteousness of God." Wasn't the goal of parenting to raise kids to love God and to gain a heart that loved and did what was right? My anger only undermined that. I know the Holy Spirit took that verse and carved it on my heart and mind. I found I became more intentional to find God's words to teach God's ways. It took thought. One principle at a time, taught and explained, established a healthier foundation for my kids. I had to have a plan, together with my husband, to train and correct. We needed to make doing what was right, a response out of loving what was right.

I want to give you a small sample of some of God's thoughts on speech. I found memorizing some of these verses gives the

Holy Spirit a tool to get my attention. Memorize them with your children. "But sanctify (set apart) Christ as Lord in your hearts, always being ready to make a defense to everyone who asks you to give an account for the hope that is in you, yet with gentleness and respect." (1 Peter 3:15)

My sister, Helen, reminded me how my mom often said, "A gentle answer turns away wrath, but a harsh word stirs up anger." (Proverbs 15:1) "The soft tone can turn a disagreement to a discussion." Mom would say, "I would rather bite my tongue than hurt others with my words." A related phrase my family has heard many times, "It is not what you say; It is how you say it." The change of spirit often diminishes the heat of a conflict.

My husband has often said, "On the day you hear of a matter, deal with it." Paul said, "Do not let the sun go down on your anger." (Ephesians 4:26) Delay often causes bitterness in at least one party in a disagreement. Prepare by prayer, with fasting if possible. Pray for wisdom to know if this is an issue that requires speech. If God's reputation is at stake, it is important to speak. If it is our own reputation that is challenged, God can be trusted to defend us.

> "If you have been snared with the words of your mouth... Go humble yourself and importune (pester) your neighbor. Give no sleep to your eyes nor slumber to your eyelids." (Proverbs 6:2–4)

> "If possible, as far as it depends upon you, be at peace will all men." (Romans 12:18)

> "When there are many words, transgression is unavoidable, but he who restrains his lips is wise." (Proverbs 10:19)(One of my favorites!)

It makes no sense to try to share God's truth with someone whose heart and mind are not prepared to receive it with respect. Pray for God to prepare someone's heart and to give you His opportune moment to speak, when a person is ready to hear it. Throwing Scripture into a conflict will not guarantee someone will hear with their heart. "Is this the time? Is the place to say this?"

God says, "So shall My Word be which goes forth from My mouth; It will not return to Me empty (without fruit or effect), without accomplishing what I desire and without succeeding in the matter for which I sent it." (Isaiah 55:11) Please note how this applies for ministry and teaching, Use as much of God's own words to explain as you can, and fewer of your own thoughts and ideas. His Words have the promise of effectiveness. "But I tell you that every careless word that people speak, they shall give an accounting for it in the day of judgement." " (Matthew 12:36) "Woe to those who call evil, good and good, evil." (Isaiah 5:20)

Sometimes difficulty in communication begins when two people speak past each other. For example, one of my daughters found it hard to discuss several issues with her dad. All he could hear was her emotion, which shut down the conversation. She needed to separate her emotions about an issue before presenting her case to her dad. He could hear her heart better and process the real issues when she wrote a letter to him. He then had all the details to consider, before they spoke face to face. They both wanted to understand the issues. They just needed a tool to make that possible. This became a strategy she still uses today with other important people in her life.

Pay attention to spiritual gift tendencies as well. For example, we have a lot of "prophet" people in our family. They tend to be very "black and white" or "all or nothing" in the way they think and the way they listen. Others are more the exhorters, those who think "let's take steps in the right direction." They want to start with one issue or remedy at a time. You may find misunderstandings between the teacher, who focuses on principles, and the mercy-giver who focuses on the emotions of the people involved. Each one has something to bring to family communication. We need to value each one's contribution.

I made a big mistake early on when I tried to interfere between Dan, a "prophet," and certain kids. I thought I was being a peacemaker. Actually, I was not. They needed their dad and his unique approach to their issues. I was hindering God from using the father He had given them. I needed to trust God to reach my children's hearts because He knows best. My kids needed to learn wisdom and experience from the dad God gave them.

One last family lesson for communication is that respect is not just from child to parent. We expect children to be patient and not interrupt adult conversations. Sometimes, I found I violated the need for respect for our teenagers when we wanted them to quickly stop to hear our instructions. We needed to be equally patient with them as they closed their conversations with their friends. They could then turn to hear us. If there is a particular issue that needs addressing, we need to keep it private, no matter the age of the kids. That is a way to respect their dignity and privacy. There is a time and place for parent-child conversations. Mutual respect is a necessary practice in family communication.

Chapter 14

SEEING WITH SPIRITUAL EYES

We should all want what God wants for us, our children and the children to come. What has our Heavenly Father stated as His desire for us? Let me pick a few for us to consider.

"Turn to Me and be saved, all the ends of the earth; For I am God and there is no other." (Isaiah 45:22) It is clear that God wants us to think beyond our lives here on the earth. He has offered us eternal life with Him. We are asked to believe that He will keep His promise to honor the death of Jesus as full payment for our legal debt before Him, the Righteous Judge. Jesus died because the "wages of sin is death." He died as a substitute for each one of us. God invites us to believe, "He is faithful and righteous to forgive us our sins and to cleanse us from all unrighteousness." (1 John 1:9)

I remember thinking as a young teen that I wanted to know for sure that I was going to heaven. My confidence could not be in my own ability to drum up a strong faith, hoping I could believe well enough to make it to heaven. I knew I would fail many times over the course of my life. Therefore, faith had to be in the God who will not fail nor break His promise. He can be trusted. What a peace that comes from His declaration, "It is finished!"

I have always appreciated my dad's joy-filled faith like that of a new believer. I wanted to live with that same sweet joy. As he approached the time of his own passing into eternity, he often said that there were more of his loved ones ahead of him in heaven than those still living here on earth. He was ready to meet Jesus. What a comfort to picture him stepping into Heaven exchanging his big bear hug with Jesus! I could imagine them turning toward the crowd, which was now calling out to him, "O Hans! You're finally here. We've been waiting for you!" The phrase God seemed to lay on my heart was "This is a perpetual reunion!" One day, it will be my turn!

I want my own children to live with that same certainty that God is ready and able to forgive their sins. Jesus has paid their penalty too. If we fail to lead them to the Mercy Seat, a place of sacrifice and forgiveness, we have failed to give them the one gift that lasts into eternity. This has to be the first deposit in the Treasure Box for our families. The testimonies of generations past are already there. There is room for ours. There will be room for theirs as well.

> "I have no greater joy than this, to hear of my children walking in the truth." (3 John 1:4)

We live in a world exploding with information, with new discoveries, and with transforming technology. There is a high priority placed on striving for excellence in education and scholarship. We need to teach our children how to study and search for the truth. But what else do they need to learn?

"Grace and peace be multiplied to you in the knowledge of God and Jesus our Lord, seeing that His divine power has granted to us every-thing pertaining to life and godliness, through the true knowledge of Him who called us by His own glory and excellence." (2 Peter 1:2–3)

If we give our children nothing else, we must intentionally share with them the knowledge God provides. We must teach them to respect His Power and Wisdom and Character. This happens daily by our own words and actions. What does our life tell them about the God we serve?

I want my children to know their Heavenly Father. He pro-vides a place for us in a family, a home, and an identity as His children. A psychologist by the name of Maslow had a theory that there are three basic needs every person must have met: belonging, personal worth, and competency. His idea was that people must provide these for themselves by their own efforts. God knows what we need, and He provided for all of our needs through our relationships with Himself. He makes us know we belong by adopting us into His family.

"But as many as received Him, to them He gave the right to be called children of God, even to those who believe in His Name." (John 1:12) He calls us the children of God, children of the King, co-heirs with His Son, Jesus. This is a family that will last for eternity without strife or selfishness. What a place of shelter provided for us by The Father!

The whole emphasis on self-esteem has created a dangerous trap for our kids. Even adults are affected by critical social media posts or public pressure to meet some arbitrary standard of accomplishment, appearance, or affiliation. When even the opinion of strangers is able to destroy someone's sense of worth, we need to be equipped with a source of unconditional love. "God demonstrates His own love for us, in that while we were still sinners, Christ died for us." (Romans 5:8) He didn't demand perfection before He was willing to give His own life for ours.

We also read in (Romans 8:31–39) that nothing can separate us from the love of God. We have unlimited worth in God's eyes. We are precious in His sight!

Maslow's third basic need was competency. Dr. Dobson, in his teaching on raising children, recommends that every child needs to have something he feels capable of doing, especially as he enters the critical years of adolescence. This is something we can help a child discover. One child may have a single-minded passion, even early in life, while another may need to try multiple interests till he finds his niche. We can give all kids the gift of encouragement. They need the freedom to fail without the fear of rejection or humiliation. Many successful entrepreneurs tell us that it was through failure that they finally found what would eventually lead to success.

God uses us as parents to help in this process, but God has also provided for that sense of competency by giving spiritual gifts to each one who is part of the Body of Christ – the Church. He not only planned what He wants us to do, He sends His Holy Spirit to equip us for that work.

> "For we are His workmanship, created in Christ Jesus for good works, which God prepared beforehand so that we would walk in them." (Ephesians 2:10)

In the teaching about the body life of the church, every member is necessary and fulfills a part that makes the body function. How great to help our children find the way they can use their abilities to serve, especially where we know God blesses and leads!

"Now the God of Peace... equip you in every good thing to do His will, working in us that which is pleasing in His sight ..." (Hebrews 13:20–21)

What are some ways we might serve? Let's look at teaching as one way God equips some people to serve in the church. Some people are natural teachers. They learn something and can't wait to teach someone else. Some people like to teach one-on-one, such as mentoring or tutoring. Some like small groups, like a Sunday School class or a retreat seminar. Some teachers are really comfortable teaching from a podium to a large group of people. Teachers are accountable to God to make sure that what is taught is consistent with the truth of Scripture.

Leadership is another gift of the Spirit. Some people are natural leaders. They tend to see the need for pulling people together to accomplish a task. Spiritual leadership has the qualifier that leaders are to be servants who lead with humility. Leaders are not to lead by the desire to control nor by arrogance. There is a difference between a rancher driving a herd of cattle and a shepherd shepherding a flock of sheep. Jesus talks about the relational component between the sheep and their shepherd. The shepherd is still overseeing and leading the sheep, but they follow because they know his voice.

Here is one more example of the working of spiritual gifts in the church. If a person has a need for counsel, several people could step in to help. The exhorter may need to help a person see the ineffective steps that caused confusion or harm in his life. He may offer some steps that could be taken to change direction and lead to better choices. Another counselor may approach the individual through the gift of mercy. Rather than focusing on action, this person may focus on emotional realities and the need to rest in the forgiveness God offers. A counselee may need both, but probably not at the same session.

God brings people with different abilities into a group to accomplish the ministry He desires. He gives the gifts and sends His Spirit to prompt people to act. Unfortunately, it seems that many congregations have become more education centers. Many attend as students or spectators. God wants us to study His Word, but He also means for us to live it out. He wants us to invest in each other's lives. (See the list of gifts described in Romans 12:3–13 for more possibilities.)

God knows we all need practice. He allows us to learn as we live and to model ministry for our kids. Are these not the gifts our families from the past have given us? Let their stories be some of the gems in your Family Treasure Box. If your family's stories have not been passed down, there are still so many biographies of heroes of the faith in the Bible you can share. (see Hebrews 11). There are also stories from history, of imperfect people who also lived lives of faith. You can discover them together in your family celebrations and add them to your family conversations. Ultimately, these people from the past are your brothers and sisters in Christ – part of the family of God. (Suggestions: George Muller, Amy Carmichael, Hudson Taylor, Jim and Elizabeth Elliot, and countless others that your friends might recommend.)

Knowing God and recognizing His work requires paying attention. We all live very busy and distracted lives. If our children are going to be able to see Him for themselves, we need to intentionally point out what we are learning. There is a children's series called The Tales of the Kingdom, written by David Mains. His allegory has a person who keeps a record of "sightings of the King." We need to do that together as a family. We may need to ask, "Did you see what God did here?" "What did

God show you in that situation?" Our observations help others to see Him too.

Our children watch our lives to see what our God is like. I often have asked, "What do they learn about God by what I say and do? Can they see that I trust God to meet my needs? Do I live in fear and worry as if He is not a trustworthy source of strength?" "Do I lead my kids to pray about needs and to pray expectantly? Are they willing to take "No" for an answer? Is His plan, even financially, what I value most? What if He gives our household an abundance? Do we pray together for how He wants His provisions used?"

Paul, the apostle, said in Philippians 4:11–13, "I know how to get along with humble means, and I also know how to live in prosperity; in any and every circumstance, I have learned the secret of being filled and going hungry, both of having abundance and suffering need. I can do all things through Christ who strengthens me."

"If we have food and clothing, with these we shall be content." (1 Timothy 6:8)

After finishing two years of college, I sensed God wanted me to take a break and attend a Bible School in Minnesota. I emptied my savings account and went. I had to live day to day, just to pay for the daily expenses of life. My grandmother wrote me a letter sharing a verse she wanted me to remember, so I would look to God for His provision. I have rested on this verse often.

"And my God will supply all your needs according to His riches in glory in Christ Jesus."

(Philippians 4:19)

What a treasure to leave for our descendants! God wants us to teach contentment and gratitude. Who knows what the days ahead will bring? We need to prepare our children to turn to the One who has provided for us and will provide for them as well, in His way and in His time.

There are so many lessons each of our families will learn over time. We have unique struggles and many that are universal. Each of us gets to see God acting on our behalf, and each will have an individual testimony of the goodness of our Lord. How fun to see how many "spiritual gems" you can find over a lifetime! We get to tell His story over and over again.

Chapter 15

RUN!

I have never loved running or jogging. I have family members who feel most alive and healthy when they have a weekly running routine. There are even people who thrive on more extreme challenges like running a marathon.

What does it take to run and run well? I learned much about the commitment it takes to be a runner by watching my son-in-law prepare to run the NYC marathon several years ago. He was not only running the full distance but he was also dribbling a basketball as he ran. He ran as part of a fundraiser for an organization. He could not just throw on some athletic shoes, drink some water, and head out on his race. What preparations were required?

First of all, he asked people who had already run marathons to give him pointers and warnings about the difficulties he would face during the race. I remember one caution was to avoid running on the metal road grating, since it would hurt your feet at a time you had already run more than half the race. He was told to run on the concrete pedestrian or bike path as he crossed the bridge. Thankfully, there are all kinds of sites online where one can find lots of wise advice and testimonials to help you make good training decisions. GP worked up with a group who helped him set goals and plan his training for the months before the actual race. He had to count the cost. He had to consider the sacrifices he would have to make for months of his life. He had a goal and a plan.

One crucial element a runner needs before, during, and after the race is a support team. Your family and friends need to be ready to encourage you if you should lose motivation. Those friends and family members get to be there on race day, cheering you on and making sure you have what you need as you run. You can even have some friends jump into the race to run with you for a portion of the marathon. It could be easy to overlook having people to help you at the end of the race when you are exhausted and in need of food and water and help as you cool down and recover.

One key part of your preparation is having the right gear for your event. Every sport has equipment and shoes and a uniform, which are required for being part of a team. My husband, Dan, has often told a story about his running days in elementary school. He had gone to school as usual on one spring day. When he got to his classroom, he found out he was supposed to be ready for a school picnic, which included the usual track and field and running events that were part of meeting the Physical Fitness requirements. Dan loved to run and was really very fast. He usually won his events, so he was excited to compete. For some reason, other kids were passing him by, which confused him. After a disappointing race, he sat down to rest. That's when it finally dawned on him. He had worn leather boots to school that day and not athletic shoes. Having the right gear could have made a big difference.

The Apostle Paul in Hebrews 12:1 describes the spiritual life as a race. "Therefore, since we have so great a cloud of witnesses surrounding us, let us also lay aside every encumbrance (impediment or burden) and the sin which so easily entangles us, and let us run with endurance, the race that is set before us." How is the life of faith a race? There is a designated route and timing for the event. God knows the number of days of our life "even before there was one." He also prepared "works that we should do" to accomplish His goals throughout our lives. There is definitely an end. "It is appointed for men to die once, and after that comes the judgement." (Hebrews 9:27)

There is a goal, a finish line which is the judgement seat of God. This is not a fearful place when you know your sins are forgiven. There is a place prepared for us in Heaven. In this case, we are eager to reach the finish line. For those who have not yielded to God's offer of forgiveness, there is only a reckoning for deeds, words, and even thoughts. There will be no place to hide when standing before the God who knows all things. In this case, a person will not run eagerly to the finish line. Instead, there will be avoidance and anxiety as the race draws to its close.

Thankfully, we know that as long as a person has breath, God is inviting every person to find peace with Him. Remember the thief on the cross who made a "deathbed" appeal. Jesus said to him, "Today you will be with Me in paradise." God wants all men to be saved and to come to the knowledge of the truth.

Obviously, in keeping with this race analogy, we too need preparation, training, and a good support team. God works in our hearts through His Word, giving us His plan for the life we are to lead. His Spirit transforms us, preparing us to be spiritually healthy so we can "run." Our training is on the job, daily serving and growing in our relationship with Him. The more we see life through His eyes, the easier it is to do what He asks.

The support team is the church and the family into which we have been placed.

When I think of running a race, I am reminded of an Olympic runner, Eric Lidell. There was a movie called "Chariots of Fire" that made his story famous. Eric Lidell was a Christian who ran in the 1924 Paris Olympic games. He was famous for taking a stand to keep the Sabbath and would not run in the events that were held on Sunday. It forced him to have to run events he had not trained to run. He often said, "God made him for China," which was his real passion in life. He had grown up in China as a son of missionaries. He and his brother were sent to a boarding school in London. He later attended Edinburgh University where he was known as a runner and a preacher. After the Olympics, he finally went to China as a missionary. He later was imprisoned in a concentration camp, where he lived as a Christian in a dark, evil world. He brought hope in the midst of the horrors of that place. He later died in that camp. He finished the race of his life, faithful to his God. A line from the movie is what most of us remember, "God made me fast, and when I run, I feel His pleasure." Those weren't really his words, but it did reflect how he lived.

"Don't you know that in a race all the runners run, but only one gets the prize? Run in such a way as to get the prize. Everyone who competes in the games exercises self-control in all things. They do it to receive a perishable wreath, but we, an imperishable." (1 Corinthians 9:24-25)

During the original Olympic games, people ran for the pleasure of Caesar. He was seen as the god of the games. They gave all they had to bring him honor. Today, we would say we need to run "All In" for God.

My daughter Mary loved to run. She joined the cross-country team at a local high school and ran shorter distance events during the track season in the spring. I remember watching her run, and she was fairly fast. She was trying to pace herself so she had something left to give at the end. She usually came in, in the top three or four runners. I remember hearing her question herself that maybe she should just give it all she has from the very beginning.

I want to be able to face my God and King, to run so as to give Him honor. I don't want to end my race knowing I held back from giving my all. I believe God invests His principles and gifts throughout our lives and that He expects us to reinvest them into those who are part of our sphere of influence. That means our children and grandchildren should hear and receive what God has given us. There are also people younger than us, often in physical age, but also in spiritual age, for whom we are responsible to help and teach. Titus 2 tells older women to teach younger women how to love their husbands and children and to be reverent in their behavior. Our busy lifestyles make this investment in the lives of others difficult. It really takes deliberate action to make those connections.

As I think about parenting, we try to give our children what each circumstance requires, day after day, year after year. We have seasons of fatigue and even discouragement. Having that support team is crucial especially in these difficult times. God asks us to run so as to win. His grace and strength are sufficient for us. Our job is to keep telling the story of who our God is and what He has done. In a way, we are running a relay race and are passing the baton to our kids. It takes practice and often requires picking up a dropped baton. Persevere.

Hebrews 11 is a chapter that places the lives of many people of faith before us to remember how they lived, or ran their races. These were flawed people with sin like the rest of us, but they believed God and God recognized their faith. Hebrews 12 reminds us that "we are surrounded by such a great cloud of witnesses ..." so run! These witnesses can testify that God was faithful to keep His promises. We need to run our race with the same confidence in Him. Our testimony to His faithfulness will be what spurs on our children and future descendants to live and RUN! Leave your stories, your testimony in your own Family Treasure Box. Those stories will be the source of hope and encouragement for generations to come. God has set the race before you, so run till you have nothing left. Run for the Glory of God!

CPSIA information can be obtained
at www.ICGtesting.com
Printed in the USA
BVHW040428170421
605186BV00005B/6

9 781662 815218